MEETING BRUCE SPRINGSTEEN

and Other Tales of Debauchery

Paul DiSclafani

Copyright © 2024 by Paul DiSclafani

All rights reserved.

Published by Red Penguin Books

Bellerose Village, New York

Library of Congress Control Number:

ISBN

Print 978-1-63777-634-6

Digital 978-1-63777-633-9

No part of this book may be reproduced in any form or by any electronic or mechanical means, including information storage and retrieval systems, without written permission from the author, except for the use of brief quotations in a book review.

The stories in this book are dedicated to the friends we've made, the friendships we've been lucky enough to maintain, and the friends we've lost.

Greg "The Big Man" Higgins
Douglas Dower
Kerri Barr

Miami Steve Van Zant wrote a great song for Southside Johnny and the Asbury Jukes called "It's Been a Long Time" (you should Google it). It's a sentimental and reflective look back by three lifelong friends (Steve, Southside, and Bruce Springsteen), reminiscing about their lives together in Asbury Park, New Jersey. The music video was shot at the epicenter of the Jersey Shore music scene, The Stone Pony.

It tells the story of their lives growing up together and their plans for the future. The chorus encourages us to raise a glass to lost comrades. When we'd hear the song at a backyard bar-b-que or anytime we were together, it became a group sing-along. Now, whenever I listen to it, it makes me sad to think about those that are gone.

My friends, it's been a long, long time...

CONTENTS

Introduction	xi
PART ONE Spirits in the Night – Meeting Bruce Springsteen *(September 1978)*	1
PART TWO Crawling from the Wreckage – Super Bowl Weekend in Pennsylvania *(January 1979)*	35
PART THREE And So It Goes – The Excommunication of Jeff Luft *(February 1979)*	75
PART FOUR It's Hard to be a Saint in the City – Studio 54 and the Wino *(April 1979)*	109
PART FIVE Five Miles to the Turnpike – The Tale of the White Whale *(May 1979)*	131
PART SIX Meeting Across the River – The Night Matty Almost Bled to Death *(February 1982)*	161
Epilogue	193
About the Author	205
Also by Paul DiSclafani	209

After a couple of minutes, what we thought was a warehouse door swung open, and Bruce Springsteen walked out.

He wore a tan and brown checkered flannel shirt over a white T-shirt. Springsteen's hair was neatly combed straight back while sporting a five o'clock shadow. With a smile stretched from ear to ear, he waved as the waiting group of girls rushed to greet him. He doled out some hugs and cheek kisses before engaging in conversation.

After chatting for a few minutes, he turned towards us.

Mother-fucking Bruce Springsteen, the Boss, right in front of us, smiling.

He greeted us with a "hello!" and reached out to shake a hand.

INTRODUCTION

It was the late '70s, and my friends and I were in our early twenties.

We were a close-knit group, spending an enormous amount of time together, mostly having a good time. It was a time to cut loose, try anything, and worry about tomorrow next year. We all knew adulthood was just around the corner, and we weren't about to pull the plug any earlier than we had to. If you and your friends also came of age during this period, you'll understand what these stories represent.

Either way, I'm sure you'll get a chuckle or two.

First, let me assure you that the events chronicled in these tales of debauchery are true. We really did meet Bruce Springsteen outside The Palladium in Manhattan. My friend Matty almost bled to death while we were celebrating my birthday in a New York City bar. On a road trip in my brother's van (we called it "The White Whale"), we installed a beer keg inside for the long haul to New Jersey.

Once, we tried to get into Studio 54, winding up so wasted that I thought the cabbie turned into a lizard. Oh, yeah, there was the time we went to the Pocono Mountains for Super Bowl weekend and, after a trip to the Emergency Room, got kicked out and drove home in a snowstorm with a car that was losing power.

Did I mention the time we traveled to Staten Island to see Southside Johnny and the Asbury Jukes at a place called The Factory,

INTRODUCTION

where we encountered people snorting cocaine off the surface of pinball machines?

There was a classic *Honeymooners* episode in which the gang tried to recapture their youth by roller skating. After they failed miserably in their attempt to be young again, Ralph Kramden paraphrased a quote from George Bernard Shaw about how youth is wasted on young people. But then he said something that has always stuck with me: The secret to staying young isn't trying to act young.

"If you've got some memories, some good memories of when you were young, that's what keeps you young. Think about it in your old age, when you were a kid, and all the things that you did. That's the whole secret to it."

Ah, yes. The stories of our youth.

A few years ago, I got together with my friends to watch a ballgame, and we reminisced about our "Glory Days." One thing led to another and the results can be found between the covers of this book. Each one contributed their recollections of different details the others forgot as we laughed and wondered how we ever survived these debacles.

With the help of my friend Bruce (Mr. B), his memory of details (so much better than mine), and plenty of notes, I pieced everything together to make these stories come to life again.

Storytelling has been going on since the beginning of time. I'm sure there was a time when caveman Grog returned from the hunt and told the story to his tribe about how he and his friends, Khorc and Gruv, captured a wooly mammoth, only to have Khorc fall into a giant pile of mammoth shit. Oh, the laughs!

I'd like to think of myself as a modern-day Grog.

Many of the people you will meet have been (and still are) dear friends for over 40 years. Some, unfortunately, have passed, which may or may not have been the impetus for finally detailing these stories as a tribute to what they meant to me in my life. Also, who knows what details any of us will remember ten years from now?

During these years, we spent most of our waking hours in each other's company. We had numerous adventures, but sometimes, we didn't have to do anything but grab a drink and talk. As we grew into

INTRODUCTION

adults with families, our contact became limited to special outings like birthdays, concerts, or ballgames. But every time we got together, we picked up where we left off without missing a beat.

Before you dive into the stories, I thought you might want to meet some of the characters that have been part of my life for all these years.

BRUCE (MR. B)

You won't find a story (or adventure) in my life as a young adult that doesn't include Mr. B, my partner in crime (so to speak). I met him in the high school chorus. He sat behind me in the Acapella Choir and was a senior when I was a nerdy sophomore. It turned out we had several mutual friends who were juniors, and we kind of hit it off.

He was always the John Lennon to my Paul McCartney, the yin to my yang. We had a memorable vacation to the West Coast with my cousin Sal the Catman, chronicled in my first book, *Burning Through the West Coast*. We even began our careers as IT Healthcare Professionals, working together for the New York City Health and Hospital Corporation. Although we always seemed to know where "the line" was, Mr. B showed me that you can occasionally put a toe across and get away with it.

GREG (THE BIG MAN)

Greg was sometimes bigger than life—and bigger than any of us. You will find him in every story in this book except one because he was on vacation in California then. Whereas Mr. B and I might occasionally put a toe across the line, The Big Man shoved us over it, along with himself.

He was a great athlete and a physical presence on our flag football team. He could hit a softball a mile. You

INTRODUCTION

always felt safe when he was around, but you also knew to expect the unexpected. Concerts, sporting events, bar hopping, golf, Fantasy Football, backyard parties—nothing got started until The Big Man showed up.

Sadly, he passed away in January of 2024.

Along with Bruce and our other friend George (The Sav), he was part of our "Core Four," who had been getting together for lunch and the occasional outing since they all retired a few years ago. When I retired in January 2024 (just before The Big Man passed), we looked forward to meeting more regularly now that we had the time.

He had an infectious, devilish smile that we will never forget.

THE DOWERS

How can one family be entrenched in so many of these stories? We met Douglas and his sisters Barbara and Susan at a local bar in Massapequa called Jocelyn's, which became our home base. Their friend, Kerri, was also part of our small circle of friends. Although we had numerous memorable adventures with Douglas as a solo artist, some of the stories in this book include the girls.

Doug Dower

Since we were all fans of the same type of music, many of our adventures together involved a Bruce Springsteen or Southside Johnny concert. However, the one adventure involving all the Dower siblings, their parents, and Kerri had nothing to do with music. It was all about a ski trip in the Poconos.

Barbara Dower

You'll find Douglas as a featured player in most of these stories. Although not as gregarious as The Big Man, he was more like Norm from Cheers. One of the funniest people on the planet and always

INTRODUCTION

made us laugh. You looked forward to his arrival at any event. He had a wealth of practical knowledge and loved cars.

We lost Douglas in November of 2020. We also lost Kerri to cancer a few years before that.

After Doug passed away, I talked with Barbara, who told me something I would never forget. While Doug was in the hospital, she brought him a copy of *Burning Through the West Coast*.

Kerri Barr

Besides making him laugh aloud, he kept reading some of the passages to the hospital staff, laughing along the way and proudly telling them, "These guys are my friends."

And what a friend he was.

MY BROTHER TONY

Tony is four years younger than me but easily integrated into our circle of friends. Maybe working with Douglas Dower for a few years at Brunswick Hospital in Amityville when he was a kid corrupted him a bit, but who knows?

Of course, us sneaking him into bars at 16 was probably not good career advice, either.

JOHN COLQUHOUN

John and I became friends at New York Tech. Although I never asked him (and he never corrected me), I always pronounced his name Cal-Houn. I was the sports editor, and he was an illustrator who eventually

INTRODUCTION

ascended to editor of *The Campus Slate*. Surprisingly, you will find him popping up as a character in a few of these stories.

As a professional illustrator, he made his bones nationally, developing beloved cartoon characters like the "pizza, pizza" guy from Little Caesar's Pizza. He also worked with Wendy's and The Outback Steak House.

I'm proud to say his illustrations for *Burning Through the West Coast* are worth the price of purchase.

John, a long-suffering Mets fan, is also a huge Southside Johnny fan.

INTRODUCTION

MATTY WYNN

Like Bruce, I've known Matty since high school. A real fireplug, you will never find a more loyal, dedicated friend. There aren't too many people who would actually take a bullet for you, but Matty is one of them. He had many credos in life (we would call them "Matty Wynn-isms"), but my favorite was always his thoughts on getting into a fight with someone, "If you want to fight, that's fine, but you better kill me…"

THE OTHERS

L-R: Bob Bochicchio, Peter Oehler

In these tales, you'll meet other characters that pop in and out along the way. There's Bruce's brother, Peter the Mooch, and our good friend Bob Bochicchio. Of course, there was also Jeff Luft, who went from hero to zero in the story "And So It Goes: The Excommunication of Jeff Luft."

At the end of *Burning Through the West Coast*, I promised my readers that I would someday tell other stories of our adventures in debauchery. The stories in this book were some of our favorites, and I hope they will be some of your favorites, too.

So sit back, grab the adult beverage of your choice, and take a trip back in time with us…

PART ONE

SPIRITS IN THE NIGHT

Meeting Bruce Springsteen

(September 1978)

CHAPTER 1
RECON AT ROOSEVELT FIELD

Bruce Springsteen was finishing up the New York leg of his mammoth 1978 tour in September. With the release of *Darkness on the Edge of Town* in June, Springsteen and the E Street Band performed 119 concerts in 222 days.

Early on, he scheduled only one show in our area, sneaking in a concert at Uniondale's Nassau Coliseum in the first week of June, between shows in Maryland and Ohio. Although the tour started in May, the album wouldn't be released until June 2nd, the day before the Uniondale show. When the tickets went on sale in April, my friend Bruce (Mr. B) and I slept out in the Roosevelt Field Mall parking lot near Macy's, which contained a Ticketron. Back then, that was the only way to get tickets for concerts and sporting events.

The day before the tickets went on sale, we did recon to scout out the location of the Ticketron machine inside Macy's. We found it upstairs next to customer service and plotted the most efficient way to get there. Using an outside entrance around the back of the building, we could zip through the perfume department, make a quick left, and up the escalator. Ticketron was to the right.

We spent Thursday night in Mr. B's car, which we nicknamed the Dent Mobile, listening to Springsteen tapes and, of course, smoking copious amounts of weed and drinking beers. Thank goodness my wristwatch has a built-in alarm. Macy's typically opens at 9:30 in the morning, but our recon paid off in spades when an employee told us they would open the outside entrance at 9:00 to accommodate the ticket buyers.

Armed with the money collected from all our friends, we stood poised to purchase those precious eight tickets, taking advantage of the four-ticket limit per person.

By 8:30 the following day, we awoke from a dead sleep (we might have passed out, who knows?) to find several other ambitious people gathering outside. Stinking of weed, beer, and body odor, we joined the growing group. About 20 or so people milled around by 9:00, waiting for the doors to open. We positioned ourselves close to the door.

In desperate need of a shower and wearing yesterday's clothes, we engaged in a happy conversation with some people, easing our way closer to the door almost imperceptibly. Once that door opened, it would be a full-out sprint.

When a Macy's employee approached the door to unlock it, about five or six people stood between us and Nirvana. Mr. B, who ran track in high school, had speed. I would be his lead blocker.

With his eyes fixed on the set of keys jingling in the woman's hand as she struggled to find the right one for this door, Mr. B whispered out of the side of his mouth in my direction. "You ready?"

I returned a slight nod. In a way, I felt sorry for the people ahead of us, knowing they would soon be behind us in a cloud of dust and body odor.

As the door swung open, the handful of people in front of us moved inside as if they were going into church for Sunday service, blocking the aisle. Mr. B tried to zig-zag to the left around them, but to no avail. I decided to break through them, but Mr. B beat me to it, cutting to the inside and pushing through. I followed him, and we were on our way!

It took the others a few precious seconds to recognize what was happening, and they, too, began running. But at this point, they were eating our dust.

With only a neatly polished tile floor in front of us, we zipped through the perfume department and took the escalator two and three steps simultaneously. Once at the top, only daylight stood between us and the Ticketron area! We sprinted around customer service and screeched to a halt, finding some people already on the line. They turned out to be Macy's employees getting a jump on us regular folks.

At least we were the first of the regular folks.

We waited patiently for our turn and quickly secured our tickets. Due to the four-ticket limit per person, we needed to purchase two sets in different sections. It didn't matter; we would all be in the Nassau Coliseum together, sharing an experience that would be the first of many.

CHAPTER 2
THE SUMMER OF '78

The summer of 1978 began with a bang.

Although the Springsteen concert was on Saturday, June 3rd, we skipped work the Friday before and went on a road trip to Six Flags Great Adventure in New Jersey. It would be a full day of fun at the amusement park, topped off with two performances by Southside Johnny and the Asbury Jukes in their Great Arena. Six Flags experimented with a series of concerts with local bands and brought in the Jukes for New Jersey's Senior Night. The shows were free to anyone with paid admission.

We piled six of us into my Chevy Nova and spent most of the day enjoying an excessive amount of time in the parking lot, drinking beer and smoking weed. We were already cooked when the Jukes took the stage in the early evening.

Of course, the ride home from Great Adventure turned into an adventure. We somehow took the wrong exit and ended up in lower Manhattan, snaking our way to the 59th Street Bridge, so we didn't pay another toll. It took us over three hours to return to Massapequa from Great Adventure, which typically takes about two.

The next night, I saw Springsteen for the first time.

Nothing could prepare me for the energy he brought that night, hooking me forever. I was also happy to find something that interested my group of friends.

We were a tight-knit circle, forming a close bond that would span our lifetimes. There was Greg (The Big Man), my brother Tony, all the Dower siblings (Doug and his sisters Barbara and Susan), and their friend, Kerri Barr.

Although we bonded over shared interests and enjoyed each other's company in bars and parties, this was different. Springsteen provided a shared experience that became the cornerstone of our friendship. We weren't groupies following him from show to show. Some people will tell you they have seen him hundreds of times. No, we chose our shows carefully over the coming years, catching Springsteen when he came to town or at a college within driving distance. My indoctrination to the road trip came during the summer of 1978.

After that single concert in June, Springsteen's tour wouldn't return to the New York area until later in the summer. Mr. B and I secured tickets for one of the Madison Square Garden concerts (8/22/78) right after we returned from our epic West Coast trip. The newspaper strike in New York City had just ended, and he opened with a song Elvis Presley made famous called "Good Rocking Tonight," changing the opening lyrics to "Have you heard the news?"

Three days later (8/25), we traveled to the War Memorial Coliseum in New Haven, Connecticut. We met a friend of Douglas Dower's, Hines, who invited us back to his apartment complex. There, we continued to party and would crash overnight. Sometime after midnight, we went out into the courtyard to play football.

During a kickoff return, I was the lone defender between the goal line and a runaway freight train named Larry Kraemer barreling down the sidelines. At twice my size, standing before a moving Kraemer in any situation was probably a bad idea. I waited until he got within a few inches of me and threw a hip check, as I've done many times while playing ice hockey.

My plan worked perfectly as Kraemer went ass over tea kettle like a whirlybird.

Except I couldn't move.

I hurt my hip to the point that it froze in place. I found out later that I suffered a hip pointer. I hobbled off the field and spent the next couple of days in pain.

But that didn't stop me.

The following night, Saturday, we attended Southside and the Jukes at My Father's Place in Roslyn. It's a small, intimate hall with long rows of 30-inch tables set up perpendicular to the stage, surrounded by seats on both sides. Halfway through the show, everyone tried to dance to the music, but there wasn't much room in the aisles, so we made room.

We stood on top of the tables, and, as difficult as that was for me in my condition, we were rocking and rolling. I was a trooper, not letting a little thing like a hip pointer slow me down.

Then, the table collapsed.

To say I saw stars would be an understatement. Nothing that more alcohol wouldn't cure, at least for now. I'm unsure if I spent the next few days recuperating from all the concerts or the hip injury.

Trekking up to Syracuse and the War Memorial Auditorium, we attended another Springsteen show on September 12th. Douglas attended school there, so we spent the night in his dorm. Since Syracuse was a dry town after 1:00 am, Doug got a ride from one of his friends to procure beer and pizza after the show. We waited outside the arena for them to return.

When he returned, we unloaded the pizzas and a few cases of beer onto the sidewalk just as Springsteen's tour bus pulled out of the underground parking lot and stopped across the street from us. Clarence Clemens leaned out his window and signaled us to give him a slice. We ran to them to share some slices without thinking, leaving the beer unguarded. Someone absconded with it.

Bummer.

Although we would take one more road trip that year for a show in Ithica in early November, we had an unexpected encounter with The Boss just after the bus incident in Syracuse, on September 16th, at The Palladium in New York City...

CHAPTER 3
THE NEW YORK INSTITUTE OF TECHNOLOGY

I was the sports editor of *The Campus Slate*, the weekly student newspaper for the New York Institute of Technology, located in Old Westbury. When I transferred to Tech after completing my associate degree at Nassau Community College, I was the lone sportswriter for the *Slate*. Quickly and without fanfare, I became the sports editor. Apparently, nobody else wanted the job.

Although the campus served technology geeks, Tech somehow managed to field teams in many competitive sports, like football, baseball, basketball, soccer, and tennis.

It was Saturday, September 16th, and both the football and soccer teams were hosting games simultaneously. Since it was very early in the semester, I hadn't recruited additional sportswriters for the *Slate*. That left Jim Gherardi, who also doubled as the photography editor, and me to cover all the sports. Jim was the interim sports editor before I took over.

He offered to write the football story since he was already taking the pictures, leaving me to cover soccer. However, no other photographers were available to take game shots.

"Why don't you shoot some pictures?" he asked me. "You got a camera?"

I owned a 35 mm camera, and although I'd never shot a sporting event before, I worried about taking action pictures and compiling notes for my article at the same time.

"Don't worry," Gherardi said, "You'll be fine. Take a bunch of pictures when everyone is standing still, and that will work."

"You dickwad," I told him, "What if I miss the game-winning goal?"

"So, you take a picture of the celebration."

"Listen, man. You take a hundred shots, hoping for one good one. I don't even have any film."

"Stop by the *Slate's* office, and they'll give you a roll of black and white."

"They better," I said. "I'm not paying for it."

I always enjoyed commuting from my Massapequa home on the south shore to New York Tech in Old Westbury, on the north shore, just west of the CW Post campus. I chose the scenic route, filled with mansions set so far back that they were not visible from the winding, tree-lined roads. The tall shrubbery and stone walls opened only for long, gated driveways. The winding asphalt of Wheatley Road would lead you to Whitney Lane, which splits between Tech and CW Post once you reached Northern Boulevard.

It was an excellent route for getting high without much traffic and no stop signs or lights. The Wheatley/Whitney part of the trip lasted about 10 minutes, roughly enough time to fire up a joint and finish it by the time you got to the campus. You weren't on the road long enough to be driving while stoned. I lit up a fresh doobie for myself, but only finished half of it, stashing the roach in my shirt pocket.

Tech was a commuter school located on sprawling grounds. It was one of the few affordable four-year colleges on Long Island and within my price range and driving distance.

The *Campus Slate* office was in the basement of a staff building adjacent to a tiny parking lot. Navigating the stairway required a certain amount of concentration, stoned or not. The landing at the bottom of the concrete steps would flood when it rained, and consequently, the place usually stunk of mildew. Since my desk was closest to the door, I had the best access to the aroma.

Upon arriving at about 10:30, I was alone and found a roll of black-and-white 35 mm film placed on my desk. The overhead fluorescent lights were on, so someone had been there earlier. I grabbed the yellow and black canister and carefully wound the film into my camera.

Turning to leave, I spotted the little red light outside the darkroom door illuminated, so one of the photographers must have been inside developing pictures. Knocking on the door, I issued a generic "Thanks for the film." With no idea who was behind the door, I heard a muffled voice return, "No problem."

Walking across the campus on this brisk end-of-summer morning, I decided to augment the sunshine and slight breeze by lighting up the second half of that joint. Getting down to the last few centimeters, I took one last hit before dropping the roach onto the pavement and snuffing it out like a '50s detective in a black-and-white movie.

Honestly, keeping track of the game events and taking photographs was daunting. In retrospect, I probably shouldn't have lit that roach on my way across campus, but you can't go back in time, right? With no zoom lens, I would have to go down from the stands now and then to shoot some ground-level pictures.

The soccer team took care of Pace University, 4-0. Afterward, I spent a few minutes with the coach and some players, then headed back to the *Slate* and banged out the story on my trusty Underwood desktop typewriter. Knowing I needed to be at work by 4:00 pm, I wasn't about to waste another minute of this weekend writing about freaking soccer.

While working on the article, one of the new photographers came into the office. I recognized his face but had no idea what his name was. If I ever copped to a character flaw, it's my severe inability to remember faces and names. I make excellent use of the "Hey, Chief" or "Hey, Buddy" cliché greetings without any idea of the person's name.

"How you doin'?" I said as he headed to the darkroom door.

"Okay," he said back. "Did you find the film I left on your desk this morning?"

I took the film canister from my pocket and tossed it across the room.

"Here you go, Chief," I said as he surprisingly made a nice catch before opening the door. "Hope there's something useable."

A few minutes later, he stuck his head out, inviting me to come in and view the developed negatives. Having never been in a darkroom, I found it somewhat intimidating and claustrophobic. That said, some of the pictures I took were freaking awesome!

"Not bad," he said, critiquing my work. We chose a couple to print and accompany the article. I shook his hand and thanked him. "Do you want another roll of film?" he asked as I returned to my desk.

"You got any color film?" I asked.

"Nope," he said. "Just black and white. We can't develop color with this equipment."

"Nah," I said. "Maybe next time."

After finishing the game summary, I grabbed my camera and threw it on the front seat of my 1975 Chevy Nova, which I lovingly nicknamed The Machine, and drove back to Massapequa. A quick check of my watch made me realize I would have to haul ass if I wanted to make it to work on time.

I never did find out that photographer dude's name.

CHAPTER 4
THE SURPRISE ROAD TRIP

During college, I worked as the shoe guy for a junior sportswear store in Massapequa's Sunrise Mall called Pants Place Plus. We had a small women's shoe department in the rear. Our clothing line ranged in sizes from 0 to 10, so most female shoppers were reasonably well put together. Along with my friend Patrick and the store manager Jim, we were the only dudes in the store.

For a young college student, this was a dream come true.

Most of my friends also had jobs in the Sunrise Mall. The Sav sold shoes in Macy's while Mr. B, Susan Dower, and Kevin "Slim" Gerlitz were downstairs at the Dime Savings Bank. My cousin, Sal the Catman, sold toys at Playworld. The Big Man, Barbara Dower, Joe Piti, and Matty Wynn all worked at Farrell's ice cream parlor. Even my brother Tony had a job in the JC Penney restaurant. In the days before cell phones, communicating Saturday night plans took place during breaks.

Many of us worked until closing on Saturdays, which fell between 9:00 and 10:00, depending on our job. We would then meet at our "home" bar, Jocelyn's, after work and make plans accordingly.

The traffic at many retail stores in the mall slowed down around dinner time and picked up later in the evening. At about 5:30, I strolled to the cashier area to chew the fat with Julia (whom I had a crush on) and the manager, Jim Pierce. Jim excused himself from the discussion to answer the phone, so Julia and I made small talk.

Jim looked a little agitated as he hung up.

"What's up?" I asked.

Originally from South Carolina, Jim still maintained his Southern Drawl.

"Fucking corporate is a pain in mah ass. They need this Gawddanged package of reeceets and reeports bah Mondee mornin'. Aah can't put it in the mail now, so I haff-ta drive in-a Manhattan and drop it off tonight. Damn."

The corporate office for Canadian Fur Trappers shared the same block as the giant Macy's.

A light bulb must have appeared above my head.

"I'll take it for you," I offered with a smile. After all, I had no plans, and any excuse for a road trip to the city on a Saturday night was a good excuse.

His eyes then lit up.

"Really?" he said. "Ya don't mahnd?"

"Are you kidding?" I told him. "Of course, I'd do it."

"Cool," he said, handing me a stuffed white envelope with the address pre-printed on the front. "It's on 34th Street, just before ya reach Sixth Avenue. They got a huge mail drop built in-a door. Shove it in the slot, and you're done. As a matta of fact, why don't cha take off now, and lemme pay you fer the rest of the day?"

"It's a deal," I said.

And just like that, this Saturday night had a purpose.

I said goodnight and headed around the mall to check out which friends were working. Mr. B would definitely be in on the plan because the bank closed at 3:00 pm on Saturdays. The Sav, my brother, and The Catman were all on until closing. I stopped into Farrell's and found that only The Big Man punched out at 6:00. Everyone else was working until 11:00.

The Big Man didn't even bat an eye.

"I'm in. Do you know what's going on in the city tonight?"

I didn't have a clue. My plan consisted of packing a cooler full of beer, driving around for a few hours, and possibly stopping at a bar.

"Springsteen is playing at The Palladium," he said with a mischievous grin.

A small venue on Fourteenth Street in Manhattan, down by New York University (NYU), the Palladium sported about 3,400 seats configured like a large movie theatre with an overhanging balcony. With Springsteen playing there for only three nights, scoring tickets bordered on the impossible, so we never tried. One show at Madison

Square Garden held twice the number of people compared to all the Palladium shows combined.

"I'll pick you up at your house," I told him and hurried to my car.

On the way home, I stopped at Mr. B's house to confirm if he wanted in on the plan. What do you think he said?

"Let's go."

Changing into my going-out clothes (jeans, T-shirt, and sneakers), I grabbed a quick bite and tossed the cooler in my back seat. After picking up Mr. B, we headed to our favorite beer distributor on Broadway in Massapequa to visit Adolf the German. He always said the same thing (in a heavy German accent) to us every time we got to the register, "You got da proof, young man? You got da proof?"

I removed a case of cold Pabst Blue Ribbon from the refrigerator, but as we proceeded to the register, something caught Mr. B's eye.

"What about these?" he said, pointing to the Foster's Lager cans on display.

Foster's Lager, an Australian beer, came in huge 25 oz canisters. We used to call them oil cans because they resembled the quart-sized motor oil containers available at most gas stations.

"You da man!" I said. We took a case of Fosters (12 cans) and plopped them on the counter along with the Pabst and a bag of ice.

"You got da proof, young man? You got da proof?"

"Of course, Adolf!" Mr. B said happily, removing the license from his wallet.

CHAPTER 5
THE CITY

Mr. B and The Big Man

Armed with a handful of joints and a cooler full of beers, we picked up The Big Man and headed west toward the Grand Central Parkway. One of the ways into the city without paying a toll was over the 59th Street Bridge, which was accessible at the end of Queens Boulevard.

With Mr. B in the co-pilot seat, The Big Man positioned himself in the back with the cooler. He reached in and handed out the Nectar of the Gods. He would adeptly distribute the beers, alternating the pedestrian PBRs with the premium Foster's. With a limited number of Fosters to enjoy, we chose to ration those.

Cracking open the first cold one (Foster's) was always a treat. We had to sip quickly to avoid exposing the giant oil cans to the outside world. There's nothing worse than taking a sip and looking to your left only to find a police car. Mr. B cracked open his window and lit the first of many joints we hoped to enjoy this fine evening.

We were on our way.

Big Man hadn't had time for dinner, so he suggested a quick stop at the McDonald's on Queens Boulevard. We picked up burgers and fries for all of us. Once on the other side of the bridge, we traveled south on Second Avenue. We made a right at 34th Street and headed up to midtown. Unfortunately, driving was getting more challenging due to the beer and the hootch beginning to take effect.

We planned to locate Canadian Fur Trappers and the magical door with the maildrop slot, then find a spot to stop the car for a minute while delivering the envelope. From the looks of the traffic on 34th, double parking would not be an option.

Herald Square is where Broadway, Sixth Avenue, and 34th Street meet. It's a nightmare during the day and even worse on a Saturday night, and we needed a place to stop and deliver a package.

Mr. B spied the "Canadian Fur Trappers" sign on a door containing a maildrop slot. As we slowly drove past it, he pointed to the unoccupied curb at the main entrance to Macy's and said, "Pull over here. I'll jump out, and you guys circle around and pick me up."

We were halfway down the block when I pulled into the empty bus lane. Mr. B grabbed the envelope and jumped out into the night.

Unfortunately for us, the streets in midtown Manhattan were not designed to circle. Some one-way avenues and streets alternate with each block, and some don't. Although it took Mr. B only a minute to drop off the package, it took us almost 15 minutes to find our way back to him.

Of course, when we finally arrived, he wasn't there.

"What the fuck do we do now?" I asked Big Man as we slowly cruised up 34th Street again.

"Want me to get out and look for him?"

Then I spied Mr. B in the rearview mirror, sprinting toward us.

I pulled into the bus lane again until he caught up.

"You assholes!" he said, catching his breath, "I was waving at you on the corner!"

"We weren't looking for you on the corner," I told him. "I thought you would be in front of the building?"

"You guys were taking so long," he said. "I thought something happened to you, so I walked to the corner to look for your car."

"You fucking Hammerhead," I said.

With our trio back in the car, we grabbed a fresh set of PBRs, fired up a joint, and set out to find The Palladium. Once there, we would hang outside the building, hoping to hear music bleeding through the walls. It was after nine, so we had a chance to arrive in time to catch the show's second half.

CHAPTER 6
THE STRANGER AND THE PALLADIUM

The Palladium sat somewhere downtown on Fourteenth Street, but we weren't sure of the exact location. Heading south on Seventh Avenue, we hung a left and headed east. We found the entrance on Fourteenth before you got to Third.

It was impossible to miss the vast, movie-theatre-style marquee jutting out from the building and extending to the sidewalk, providing shelter to anyone below. The brightly lit sides contained red block letters pressed into place announcing, "Welcome Back Bruce Springsteen & The E Street Band."

Driving past the venue, we took a right at Third and went around the corner, cutting up Thirteenth. We were hoping to find a parking space somewhere in the neighborhood. Although there were a few garages in the area, we weren't about to spend cash to park if we didn't have to.

We got about halfway up Thirteenth Street and found a spot near a warehouse. We grabbed a fresh set of Foster's (round two) and walked around the block to the Palladium entrance.

"Listen," I said as we approached the front door, "You can hear the show from out here!"

Even with the muted sound, we recognized Springsteen's "Jungleland," which, in our experience, concluded the first set. I put my ear to the outside wall and swore I heard the music better.

"This sucks ass," Mr. B said. "We gotta get inside."

"I can't believe we're this close and can't get in," I said.

The Big Man suggested we split up and find out if scalpers were still selling tickets. The prices must have come down since the show's first half was over.

Two large, rolled-down metal gates covered most of the front of the building below the marquee. A small, rolled-up section of the gate hung over the entrance.

A small sign hung haphazardly with duct tape in the middle of the gate confirming the Sold Out event. Guarded by a monster of a security guard, only those with tickets gained admission through this entrance. He reminded those few people who left after the intermission (lightweights) of the no-re-entry policy after leaving the building. That ended my hopes of buying their tickets and trying to use them.

I ran into Mr. B on Fourteenth Street, but he also came up empty. By now, the band returned to the stage, and the muffled sounds of "Kitty's Back" leaked from the concrete walls. We trudged dejectedly back to the car to smoke a joint and grab a fresh beer.

Meanwhile, The Big Man had struck up a conversation with some dude down the block from the Palladium entrance.

"You looking to get into the show?" the stranger asks Big Man.

"Sure. Can you do that?"

"Twenty bucks, and you're inside."

"What about my friends?" The Big Man countered. "I have two friends with me."

"Sorry, pal. This is a one-shot deal for you only. I'm not sure I can get you all in."

"Well then, forget it," Big Man said. "I came here with those guys; what do you suggest I do about them?"

"Well, where are they now?" he asked. "Tell you what. I'm going to be standing right here. If you find them, come back, and I'll see what I can do."

The Big Man took off and sprinted around the block, trying to find us. We were leaning against the car with some PBRs and sharing a joint.

"I found somebody that might be able to get us in," Big Man said as he fought to catch his breath. "He's around the corner, but we have to go now."

We chugged the last of the beers and sped off. We found the guy on Fourteenth Street, about 50 yards from the front entrance. Short and chubby, he wore an unzipped blue windbreaker designed for a slightly more petite person. The Yankees hat on his head stretched low over his eyebrows and was a blatant knockoff you could buy at a drugstore for a buck. The interlocking N and Y tilted to the left.

The mysterious stranger chewed on the remains of an unlit cigar while acknowledging our presence with a slight nod. The Big Man did all the talking.

"Hey, pal, we're all here. Wadda ya say?"

The mystery man rotated his head from side to side, looked us over, and sighed heavily. "I can get in a lot of trouble for this, but you guys look cool. Twenty bucks apiece, and you're in."

Somehow, I got the feeling that if we were ten guys, we all would have gotten in—money talks.

"Twenty bucks!" Mr. B yelled. "That's bullshit. The second half of the show already started!"

I stepped in front of Mr. B to talk directly to the guy. "How are you getting us in?"

"See that security guard over there?" he said, gesturing to the entrance. "You go up to him and say, 'Bayonne.' He opens the door, and you're in."

"Bayonne?" I said, "Like the city in New Jersey?"

"That's right, Genius. You know any other Bayonne?"

"Are you out of your fucking mind?" Mr. B said.

"Listen, you guys are in much better shape than me and can easily run me down if he doesn't let you in. Tell you what. How about forty bucks for the three of you? Wadda ya say? We doing this, or you goin home?"

"He's got a point," I said, reaching into my pocket for cash. "I'm in."

"What do we do once inside since we don't have tickets?" Big Man asked.

"Go to the left past the concessions, and you can stand in the back or along the sides. It's like a giant movie theatre inside."

We handed over three tens and a couple of fives.

Taking our money, he reached into his pocket, pulling out a wad of folded bills. He placed ours with all the rest of the cash and stuffed them back into his pants. Catching the eye of the security guard, he gave him a discrete wave and got a small acknowledgment wave back.

"You're all set," he said. "Enjoy the rest of the show."

Approaching the front door, I was a little apprehensive. We already paid the dude, so it is what it is. I peered over my shoulder to ensure our contact was still there, and he waved, signaling us to keep going.

"This better work, or I'm going to kick this guy's ass," Mr. B commented.

I took the lead and walked up to the security guard, simply saying the magic word, "Bayonne." He moved to his left and opened the door, giving us entrance into the lobby, which housed the concessions.

The lobby retained the look and feel of an old-time movie theatre where you buy popcorn, candy, and soda. But for this show, you could also purchase T-shirts. A makeshift bar selling beer, mixed drinks, and wine was in the corner. Money was dwindling at this point, but we scraped together enough cash for a round of beers in plastic cups.

Once inside, we felt the raw power emanating from the stage in the tiny theatre while the band was performing "Candy's Room." Our previous Bruce shows had been indoor sports arenas, like the Nassau Coliseum, but this was more intimate. Two sections of movie-style seats were on the floor, split down the middle by a wide aisle with a balcony hanging overhead. The back housed a gathering space for standing and dancing, as did a six-foot area between the end of the individual rows and the side walls.

Limited to where we could stand without seated tickets, we calculated that more than 100 people were already occupying each side, with double that amount in the back. That wad of bills in the guy's pocket made more sense.

We snaked our way to the left and found a few empty spots on the wall to lean against—not that we did much leaning. If you've ever seen Springsteen live, having a seat sometimes is a complete waste of time.

At some point, someone hung a massive banner from the balcony that said, "Incident on 57th Street." Springsteen looked up, smiled, and the band launched into the song. It was a rare treat for Springsteen to perform that one live.

Although in the past, we paid much less for a Springsteen ticket and got to see the entire show, the half-show we witnessed was worth every scalped penny. The size of the venue and the acoustics provided an intimacy you can't duplicate inside a vast arena. You could feel this concert. Springsteen and his band enjoyed playing on this stage as much as we enjoyed experiencing it. We weren't just listening; we were participating.

Upon hearing the opening notes of "Rosalita," usually the last song before the encores, we rushed to the open area in front of the stage with others ahead of security, trying to intervene and stop it. However, they let those of us already there stay.

We were right up against the stage for "Rosalita" and all the encores, right in front of the real Big Man, Clarence Clemons, on the far left. Along with the rest of the crowd, we bopped to showstoppers like "Born to Run," "Tenth Avenue Freeze-Out," the "Detroit Medley," and a song by The Dovells called "You Can't Sit Down." At the show's end, the band came out to the front of the stage and reached down to give high-fives. I got to slap hands with Clarence, who was a sweaty mess!

Exiting the theatre, we couldn't stop talking about our luck and what a great experience we had. Our mystery guy and his in-cahoots security guard were nowhere to be found. I assumed they were in some bar splitting their bounty.

Approaching our car around the corner on Thirteenth Street, we noticed about 200 people gathering near the entrance of the warehouse building across from us in the small parking lot. We walked over to see what was happening and found this particular door led into The Palladium. It was the backstage entrance.

"This is where everyone comes out after the show," some chick told us. "Springsteen and the band will be coming out soon, and we're gonna get some autographs!"

Really…

CHAPTER 7
THE BOSS

While talking with the others congregating around the door, we were sure we would catch a glimpse of most, if not all, of the E Street band members. But the throng of people was a little intimidating. Even if the band exited from this portal, they weren't hanging around to give autographs to all these people.

We backed away from the crowd and decided to return to the car, view things from afar, and crack open another round of Foster's (round three). After all, we had a front-row seat to everything.

After about 30 minutes, a limo pulled up, and the building door opened. Danny Federici and Roy Bittan, Springsteen's organist and piano player, came out. The waiting crowd immediately met them, shaking hands and exchanging high-fives before getting into their rides and heading off.

The rest of the E Street Band slowly emerged from the venue into their waiting limos and car services. More than an hour after the show ended, the original crowd of adoring fans dwindled to about 30 or 40 people.

"You think he's still inside?" I asked Big Man, who was nursing the last of the PBRs.

"Well, we've been here for a long time and haven't seen him leave yet. Let's go down there and see what's going on."

Plenty of chicks were still hanging out, making it a much more pleasant experience hanging out with them instead of by ourselves. There were varying theories about why (or if) Springsteen was still in the building, but the one that made the most sense came from some random guy. He said Carol Miller from the New York City radio station WPLJ was interviewing him. He drove with his friend, an audio technician for WPLJ, who was working with Miller. He was waiting for them to finish the interview so they could go home.

"We were here last night," the hot blonde in the white-flowered top said, pointing to her two equally cute friends. "We got to meet him for a few minutes. He was so cool!"

The Big Man jumped in to ask them about the show.

"Oh no, we couldn't get tickets. We just hung out here after the show. There were a lot more people here last night. He said he was in a hurry and apologized but still signed a few autographs before he took off."

It was after midnight, and only a handful of people remained by the door, including the three chicks, waiting for Springsteen to emerge. We were not about to give up, but it became part of the discussion. A quick cooler inventory revealed one more round of Fosters and a couple of PBRs. Not that it mattered. We were cooked.

A late model, power blue Monte Carlo entered the small parking lot. A female passenger got out and went through the portal. After about ten minutes, the woman returned to the car, but they didn't leave. We found out later that it was Springsteen's sister and her husband.

We looked at each other, and Mr. B said, "You think that's his ride?"

"Could be," The Big Man said.

After a couple of minutes, the warehouse door opened, and Bruce Springsteen walked out.

He wore a tan and brown checkered flannel shirt over a white T-shirt. Springsteen's hair was neatly combed straight back while sporting a five o'clock shadow. With a smile stretching from ear to ear, he waved as the waiting group of girls rushed to greet him. He doled out some hugs and cheek kisses before engaging in conversations.

We snapped from our trance and raced across the street to join the small group.

Making his way through the few remaining fans, he recognized the three girls from the previous night.

"Hey, you made it back!"

The hot blonde produced a poster for him to sign. "I told you we'd be back. Can you sign my poster?" She handed him a black Sharpie.

As he unfurled the rolled-up poster, he looked at the picture and recoiled.

"Oh, wow!" he said as he tugged on his shirt, pointing at the image depicting him leaning against a wall wearing the same shirt. "Some wardrobe, right?"

Everyone had a good laugh.

He chatted for a few more minutes with the girls, then turned toward us.

Mother-Fucking Bruce Springsteen, the Boss, right in front of us, smiling.

He greeted us with a "Hello!" and reached out to shake a hand. Listed at 5-10, he seemed a little shorter than that. He certainly wasn't this larger-than-life performer we've seen on stage.

The Big Man reacted first and snatched his outstretched hand.

"We saw you in Syracuse the other night," he offered as his huge hand engulfed Springsteen's tiny guitarist hands.

"That was a hot show," Springsteen remarked, "We were really rocking!"

Mr. B broke out of his trance. "We also caught you at the Garden and up in Connecticut a few weeks ago."

"Wow," Springsteen said as he shook Mr. B's hand, "Thanks for supporting the band."

When it was my turn, I was star-struck. I reached out for Springsteen's hand and told him how much I enjoyed his music, especially his live shows.

"Thanks, man," he said. "I hope you'll continue to come to our shows and support the band!"

At that point, I asked him if he would wait a minute as I ran to my car for something he could sign.

"Sure," he said. "I'm not going anywhere; I'll wait."

I ran back to the car while Mr. B and The Big Man stayed with Springsteen. I had a placard on the dashboard with "Team F.U.B.A.R." on it. That would be perfect for me! I then rustled around in the glove compartment to find something for Mr. B and The Big Man. I found a few crumpled pieces of paper.

And then I saw it—my camera!

I used it for the soccer game earlier in the day, and there it was—on the floor by the passenger seat. This was great! I could take pictures of the four of us together for all the world to see!

Meeting Bruce Springsteen would be recorded forever in photogr….

OH, NO! I DIDN'T HAVE ANY FILM IN THE FUCKING CAMERA!!!!

What an asshole I was!

Earlier in the day, the photographer at *The Slate* offered to give me another roll of film, but I said no because I didn't want black and white. Now, with a chance for a personal photograph with Bruce Springsteen and, and, and…

I snapped out of my depression and ran back across the street.

I presented Springsteen with the Team F.U.B.A.R. placard and asked him to sign it "To Disco." He looked at me funny, and I said, "No relation to music, please." He chuckled as he scribbled his name.

"What's Team F.U.B.A.R.?" he asked, handing me back the placard.

"Fucked Up Beyond All Repair," I told him.

Springsteen laughed heartily, shook my hand again, and said, "I have to remember that!"

Mr. B jumped in next. He handed Springsteen the crumpled piece of paper.

"Who am I making this out to?" Springsteen asked.

"Why, Bruce, of course!" Mr. B answered.

"Is that your name?"

"Yep," as Mr. B grabbed his hand.

"What a great name!" Springsteen said, shaking his hand again.

When Big Man's turn came, he seemed a little embarrassed to ask Springsteen to sign it for "The Big Man," so he asked him to use his given name, Greg.

"Yeah," Mr. B remarked, "But we call him The Big Man."

Springsteen just smiled.

CHAPTER 8
THE CHASE

What began as a mob of over 200, only the four of us remained, like spirits in the night.

"Well, that's it for me," Springsteen said, pointing to the Monte Carlo. "My ride's here, and I gotta go. Thanks again for supportin' the band, and we'll see you again!"

We shook his hand again and watched as he headed into the back seat. We passed behind them to cross the street, and he waved to us, so we waved back.

We were higher than a kite at that point.

Sitting in my car, we were initially silent, in stunned disbelief. After staring at the placard with his signature, I noticed his ride exiting onto Thirteenth Street. Since Thirteenth was a one-way heading west, they could only go in that direction, and we were already facing that direction.

"Should we follow him?" I asked, knowing full well the answer.

"Why not?" Mr. B said while pushing the *Darkness on the Edge of Town* cassette into the player.

"Sounds like a plan," came from The Big Man as he reached into the cooler and distributed the last round of Foster's Lagers.

We cracked open the oil cans as the first few drumbeats from "Badlands" blasted from the speakers and lit up the remaining joint.

We followed behind the Monte Carlo on Thirteenth Street, making a right onto Fourth Avenue and heading north. When Fourth merged into Park Avenue, we pulled up next to them at a light and rolled down the windows so Springsteen could hear us blasting his music. When he turned to acknowledge us, we lifted our oil cans to salute him, and he shook his head laughing.

As they proceeded up Park, we caught them occasionally, sticking our heads out the window and screaming the song lyrics. We were approaching the end of Park, at 42nd Street by Grand Central Terminal. There were two options at that point: Make a left turn for the Lincoln Tunnel, following the sign indicating "To New Jersey," or make a right for the Queens Midtown Tunnel, following the sign "To Long Island."

When the Monte Carlo turned left for New Jersey, we made the bold move to follow them.

Once on the Jersey Side, Springsteen's ride traveled south on I-95. We stayed well behind it to avoid appearing to be stalking it. We discussed how far to take this and decided to go all the way and find out where he lived.

After a few miles, they pulled off I-95 into a rest stop. Like ninjas, we found a secluded area to park and witnessed them walk inside, settling into an empty window booth overlooking the parking lot. Waiting a few minutes to make it look like a surprise encounter, we casually strolled inside and passed the threesome's booth.

We greeted them with warm handshakes, and Springsteen asked us to join them. He introduced us to his sister Virginia (he called her Ginny) and her husband Michael Shave. Before we knew it, we were having casual conversations like old friends.

Springsteen invited us to join him at his house and, and, and…

Nah—we never followed them to Jersey.

After terrorizing Springsteen for 30 or so blocks up Park Avenue, we waved goodbye to him at 42nd Street (he waved back) and headed to Long Island. At the same time, the Monte Carlo sped off into the night on its way to the Lincoln Tunnel and New Jersey.

With the radio blasting the rest of the song catalog from *Darkness on the Edge of Town*, we triumphantly made our way back to Massapequa, stopping at Jocelyn's and hoping to find the others from our little gang to tell them all about our evening and what they missed.

And boy, did they miss out.

Now, if I only had photographs…

PART TWO

CRAWLING FROM THE WRECKAGE

Super Bowl Weekend in Pennsylvania
(January 1979)

CHAPTER 1
THE INVITE

We never had any intention of skiing.

But how could we pass up a road trip to a private vacation home in the Poconos on Super Bowl Weekend, which provided free room and board? It didn't matter. The others would enjoy the slopes and a lovely reunion with old friends.

We had different plans in mind.

It was getting late into the evening on the Saturday after New Year's of 1979 as we continued drinking with friends at our favorite Massapequa watering hole, Jocelyn's. Barbara Dower and her friend Kerri Barr excitedly told us about their planned ski trip for Super Bowl weekend in the Pocono Mountains. They thought we might like to join them.

"We don't have to ski, do we?" I asked innocently.

"Why not, Disco?" asked Kerri.

"I never ski," said Barbara's older brother Douglas.

"I might ski," said Greg (The Big Man).

"Is everyone else skiing?" asked Bruce (Mr. B).

Besides her parents, Russ and Eileen, Barbara knew everyone would be skiing except Douglas.

Joining the Dower clan would be the Finkernagles, their Massapequa Park neighbors who relocated to Pennsylvania a few years back. Part of maintaining their relationship was a yearly rendezvous for a weekend getaway in the Poconos, including some skiing time. Although Russ and Eileen didn't ski, they would hang out at the lodge while the others took their chances on the slopes.

With the kids getting older and wanting to bring along friends, they previously chose to stay at hotels to accommodate the growing crowd. This go-round, the families decided to rent a private house in the

Poconos, a precursor to today's Airbnb home rentals. Barbara had already seen the rental agreement and a brochure with pictures and excitedly told us about it.

The rental unit was an A-Frame house with four bedrooms, a nice-sized dining room, and an eat-in kitchen on the upper floor. The ground level sported a playroom with a pool table, a free-standing bar, a fireplace, and a television. Protected by a barrier railing, the upstairs hallway provided a perfect overview of the downstairs living space.

Guess where we would be hanging out?

Douglas sounded a little desperate. You see, Douglas had already invited his friend Lance as his "Plus One" for the trip, but Lance wanted to ski. That would leave Doug as the only non-skier on the trip besides his parents. I guess that would make us his "Plus Two, Three, and Four."

"You guys have to come. I'm the only one who doesn't ski, and I'm not spending the entire day sitting in the Lodge with my parents. We don't even have to go to the mountain with them. We'll have the place all to ourselves on Saturday."

Mr. B was a little skeptical, and his left eyebrow rose slightly. "Are you sure your father is okay with this?"

Douglas smiled and downed the remaining rat's ass of his beer, swinging his empty back and forth to catch the eye of Gary, the bartender. Gary dutifully snatched the long neck of a Budweiser protruding from the ice with one hand and twisted off the cap with the other, placing it in front of Douglas. Before the ice fragments could melt, Douglas was already mumbling as he took a swig. "Of course, he likes you guys."

That's when I heard an audible laugh from Kerri.

Neither Russ nor Eileen Dower had a clue their kids invited a few more friends to be part of their weekend getaway. Our limited exposure to their parents was picking up a slightly inebriated Douglas early in the evening or returning a more intoxicated Douglas later on.

Over the next few days, we repeatedly asked if our presence during this soiree was welcome. Douglas would always answer, "Nonsense—of course, it's okay," but we needed confirmation from Barbara.

Mr. B, Big Man, and I planned to leave for the Poconos on Friday evening, right after I finished work, putting our arrival near midnight. Once we cleared the George Washington Bridge into New Jersey, it was a straight run on Route 80 over the Pennsylvania border. The trip from Massapequa would typically take a little over two hours.

While the weather on Long Island this late in January was bitterly cold, we weren't expecting any precipitation in the Poconos until Saturday night. The forecast predicted snow and sleeting rain but clear skies on Sunday, which worked out great for us because we were heading home after the Pittsburgh-Dallas Super Bowl.

The Big Man commandeered his father's spacious and luxurious 1974 Pontiac Catalina, anchored in the driveway while his snowbird parents were on their annual trip to Florida. The dark brown two-door sedan sported a tan Cordova vinyl top spanning the back half of the passenger compartment. The car features double, side-by-side headlights and a giant trunk that would have made any Mafia boss proud. With steel belted radial tires, the Catalina drove like a dream. The tan interior boasted a single-row seat up front, power windows, cruise control, and a great radio—what's not to like?

Friday morning, we placed Mr. B's home stereo equipment into the spacious trunk of the Catalina. In addition to the electronics, there was plenty of room to store about 50 hand-picked albums from his vast record collection (over 300) housed inside two plastic milk crates.

Mr. B and The Big Man completed the necessary preparations for an entire weekend of debauchery while I finished my shift at Pants Place Plus in the Sunrise Mall. They rolled a few joints, procured the snacks, and loaded beer and ice into the cooler for the trip.

By the time I got off work, I only needed to grab my bag, and we were ready for liftoff. We were on our way across state lines with a shanghaied Catalina stuffed with stereo equipment, contraband, and a cooler full of beer.

What could possibly go wrong?

CHAPTER 2
THE ARRIVAL

The Big Man doesn't like to drive at night, so I took the wheel once we got over the George Washington Bridge. With Mr. B riding shotgun as my navigator (where have I heard that phrase before?), The Big Man settled in the back seat and distributed beers. We packed three additional cases to cover the rest of the weekend.

It took us over three hours to reach Pennsylvania and locate the house, arriving after midnight.

Approaching the chalet, I thought, *This is way too nice for us.* The light emanating from inside the A-Frame structure's enormous front windows glowed yellow against the dark backdrop of the mountains behind it.

The property contained a large, wide driveway to the right of the house, stretching a considerable distance from the front door. Four cars, including a white van, parked two by two behind each other. We barely squeezed into the narrow area at the far end of the property, which had yet to be shoveled. The rest of the driveway and walkway had been dug out at some point, but we had to park in about six inches of fresh snow.

We exited the Catalina and stretched our legs for a minute or two. Barbara came rushing out the front door with a parka draped over her shoulders, smiling and waving. However, she was signaling to us to stop dead in our tracks. Barbara's tall, athletic build complemented her flowing brown hair.

"Please be as quiet as possible. My parents and the Finkernagles are asleep, so you gotta be quiet."

With the forecast calling for freezing rain in the late afternoon tomorrow, the group's skiers wanted an early jump on their second day of skiing. After arriving on Friday afternoon, they had already done several runs down the mountain. However, the Finkernagle teenage kids were still up and looking forward to hanging out without the adults.

Tiptoeing into the house to greet everyone, we found Douglas and his friend Lance engaged in a game of pool. To the right of the green-felt table stood a free-standing bar with Kerri, and Barbara's younger sister Susan, wearing casual sleepwear of T-shirts and sweatpants and occupying two swiveling stools. Although the mirrored wall behind the bar contained a few glass shelves, no bottles of booze were waiting to be poured. Instead, a bottle of vodka and an open container of orange juice occupied the bar top. They hopped off their perches and shuffled to greet us in their fuzzy slippers.

To the left, cut into the far wall, was a fireplace and a mantle. A healthy supply of lumbered wood sat in the holder, and logs were happily burning in the andiron. A pair of matching red and tan bean bags and some comfy chairs around the perimeter seemed lonely without occupants.

To the right of the fireplace, the back corner housed a functioning TV surrounded by two brown, corduroy couches occupied by what we assumed were the Finkernagle's teenage boys. Seemingly oblivious to our presence, their dangling legs were visible over the sides.

Mr. B surveyed the room for a place to hold the equipment, eyeing the mantle. "Let's use that shelf for the stereo."

His words piqued the interest of one of the Finkernagle kids. "Stereo?"

As Mr. B and I retreated to the Catalina to unload our stuff, I noticed The Big Man lagging and chatting privately with Susan. Once outside, I nudged Mr. B and pointed to the developments inside.

"What's that all about?"

Mr. B just shrugged his shoulders. He always had a thing for Susan, but she always treated their relationship as brother and sister. Could The Big Man be secretly stepping out on Mr. B?

We began unloading the Catalina, starting with the receiver and speakers. The Finkernagle kids took it all in from the safety of their couches and smiled. Subsequent trips, with The Big Man now engaged with us, brought the rest of our gear—albums, a cooler, and a few cases of beer. I thought I detected the teenager's expression change from excitement to fear. Who are these guys, and what are they doing in our chalet?

Setting up Mr. B's stereo components took some time. Douglas cleared two pots with fake flowers and a decorative urn off the mantle to make room for the receiver. We checked the urn to ensure it didn't contain someone's ashes, but it was empty, thank goodness.

The speakers took their places on the floor surrounding the fireplace. The turntable fit nicely on the end table, meaning we had to find an alternate location for the lamp.

We toasted to our upcoming weekend and grabbed a fresh set of beers for everyone (except the Finkernagle kids). Mr. B loaded Springsteen's *Darkness on the Edge of Town* onto the platter, setting the volume to a reasonable level and being as considerate as possible of the people sleeping upstairs.

Maybe not…

Within a few minutes of the second song, Mr. Dower appeared in a robe and slippers, peering down over the railing.

"What the hell is going on down there? Turn that down right now. Jesus H. Christ, people are trying to sleep."

He then looked at the crudely assembled stereo system.

"Did you guys bring a fucking stereo? Oh, Jeez…"

He shook his head and mumbled while trekking back down the hallway. We had been there about 20 minutes and were already causing trouble.

The girls and the Finkernagle kids eventually retired upstairs while we stayed awake with Douglas and Lance. With the sound excruciatingly low, we continued to listen to tunes and shot some pool.

"My parents said if we behave, we can have a party tomorrow night," Douglas said. "Everyone will be done skiing, and we can just enjoy ourselves down here after dinner."

"Sounds like a plan," I offered. "Maybe we can get your dad and Mr. Finkel-whatever to play pool with us?"

"First of all, it's Finkernagle, you dick head," Mr. B said, "and second of all, I don't think he'll like us at all."

Big Man gave him a quizzical look. "First of all, who gives a shit what their name is? Second of all, how do you know that?"

"I met him and his wife at the Dower's house once when I was waiting for Douglas to come downstairs on our way to Jocelyn's," Mr. B said. "I heard him and Mr. Dower talking about us. He said all kids our age are assholes. He was being a real dick."

Douglas measured the five-ball to carom into the side pocket, but it missed by a mile. "I don't think they'll want to play pool with us."

Lance crashed on one of the couches, leaving us to fend for ourselves. He planned on skiing with everyone else in the morning. As the remaining beers dwindled, we refilled the cooler from our stash and continued drinking. We went outside to smoke a joint but eventually decided to call it a night sometime after 2:00 am.

CHAPTER 3
THE PRE-GAME BREAKFAST

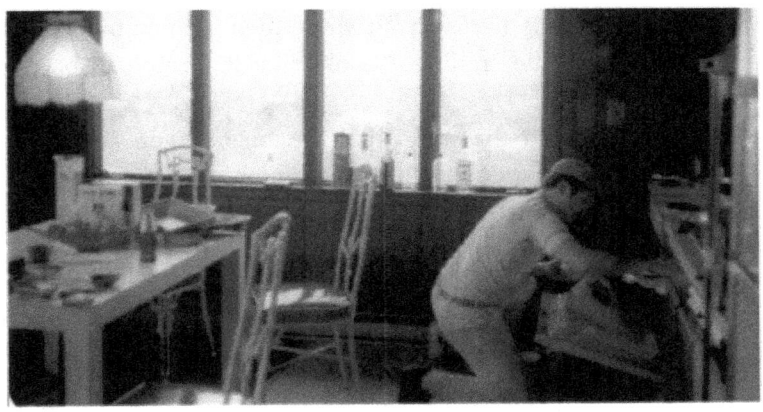

I woke up downstairs around 10:00 and found Douglas and Lance missing. Looking out the window, snow was falling, and the only cars left in the driveway, the Catalina and the white van, had a few inches blanketing their exterior. There was rustling from the kitchen, so I went upstairs to find Douglas on one knee, rummaging through the pots and pans in the lower cabinet. An Irish flat cap was covering his slightly balding head.

"Disco, how do you like your eggs?"

He had already chopped onions, and a pack of uncooked bacon was on the counter. He just needed a frying pan.

"I like them scrambled," I said.

"Excellent! That's the only way I make them."

"I guess we're not going skiing."

Smiling and taking a sip from a 16-oz beer that didn't come from our stash, Douglas methodically reached inside the fridge, procured another unaccounted-for tall boy, and cracked it open before handing it to me. "Everyone else is gone."

I took a slug and headed downstairs to change my clothes and rouse The Big Man and Mr. B, bringing them up to speed on the events going on in the kitchen. The unmistakable aroma of cooked bacon began wafting to the lower level.

The Big Man grabbed two beers from the surprisingly cold water in the cooler and playfully flung one to Mr. B, then popped the top on the other for himself while smiling. "Looks like it's going to be one of those days."

Mr. B fiddled with the radio dial on the receiver, landing on a station playing a Bob Seger song and cranking up the volume. With the music blasting and armed with fresh clothes and beers, we headed up the stairs to join Douglas for breakfast.

The galley-style kitchen stood a few feet from the staircase in the middle of the second level, sporting a rectangular table with six blue-cushioned, wire-legged chairs. A decorative bowl sat in the center, stocked with fresh fruit—bananas, apples, tangerines, and oranges. There were large windows positioned at the back end sporting a small sill containing strategically displayed bottles of liquor in varying stages of capacity, from unopened to virtually empty. The right side had the stove, fridge, sink, and countertops, while the other sported the centered dinette.

Upon exiting the kitchen, a small carpeted hallway overlooked the first-floor playroom. The bedrooms and an additional bathroom were to the left of the stairs, with a small sitting room to the right that led into the dining room.

Taking our seats at the table, Douglas began dishing out the scrambled eggs and bacon. The Big Man took a quick inventory of the bottles adorning the window sill and grabbed the open vodka, ignoring the scotch. While looking for additional plates in the cabinet, Douglas found an unopened Jack Daniels bottle. Grabbing the Jack and twisting off the top, he reached for a couple of juice-sized glasses, cracked the seal, and we had some with our eggs.

We were happily munching on breakfast when Mr. B noticed the falling snow from this morning transformed into sleet and rain. The change in precipitation would soon create an icy mess. With a mouthful of scrambled eggs, he pointed out the window, then paused to swallow.

"Well, that doesn't look good."

"Can you ski in this weather?" I asked.

"Who the fuck knows?" Douglas said.

The Big Man went to the fridge to look for orange juice to add to an already-poured half-glass of vodka, but the early morning ski crew finished it off during their breakfast.

"Damn," he said, "I was gonna make a screwdriver, all the OJ is gone."

As if on cue, Mr. B snatched an orange from the fruit bowl and fired it at him. "Use this!"

The throw sailed a little low, and The Big Man stuck out his leg to kick at it, causing the orb to veer off out of the opening of the kitchen area and down the hallway.

Immediately, a light went on in my head. I retrieved the orange and kicked it back into the kitchen. Before I knew it, Mr. B and Douglas got in on the fun, and we were kicking it around like a tiny soccer ball.

When Mr. B moved into position to kick the orange after it landed against the side wall, The Big Man charged full speed, smashing human and fruit. Falling backward onto the table, Mr. B knocked a plate to the floor, which broke into a million pieces.

Douglas found two wicker brooms inside the tall cabinet at the end of the kitchen. While he appropriated one to clean up the fragments, The Big Man removed the other, holding it like a hockey stick. He used it to take a slapshot with one of the rogue apples in my direction. Standing near the doorway, I instinctively crouched into a goalie stance as Big Man fired away.

The apple puck flew across the linoleum, but I routinely made the kick save as it disappeared under the table. While trying to retrieve it from between the tangle of chair legs, we made an executive decision to remove the table and chairs, creating a much larger playing surface.

With fresh beers (and another shot or two of Jack), we began a game of floor hockey using produce and brooms we would soon grow to regret.

CHAPTER 4
THE GAME

I teamed up as a goalie with Mr. B, who took Douglas's broom. With The Big Man wielding the other broom as a weapon, Douglas took his position as a goalie, guarding the opening into the hallway. I took my place in front of the windows at the other end. We cleared the counters of all appliances and knickknacks so as not to break anything else. Soon, we were in full-on, smashmouth floor hockey—with brooms and fruit.

Of course, Mr. B comes in a much smaller package than The Big Man. His low center of gravity and quickness help him escape most harrowing situations. However, there was plenty of carnage as the game went on. Each time a piece became unplayable, we took another. And another. And another.

For the record, oranges are more durable than apples or tangerines. The apples appeared rugged enough to take some early pounding but bruised easily before turning to mush. A tangerine is lighter and flies through the air, but the outer skin is fragile and tears easily, causing little wedges to explode in all directions. It's a good thing we had plenty of tangerines to work with.

Soon, the once pristine floor became littered with pieces of smashed apples and tangerine slices. To make matters worse, the wicker bristles of the brooms were beginning to tear off, joining the fruit remnants. Not that anyone was keeping score, but Mr. B and I were winning this particular contest. We would take a break every five or ten minutes, fix ourselves a drink, and then continue.

As expected, Mr. B took a beating against the hard-checking Big Man. We would switch off occasionally so I could absorb some of the punishment. Anything for a friend, right? Douglas, however, stayed anchored as a goalie, wanting no part of the action happening in the middle of the kitchen. Besides, if he were holding a broomstick, he wouldn't have been able to keep drinking while play continued.

During one much-needed break, Mr. B headed downstairs and switched off the radio to load a record. Using the end of an album side as our timer, the rest of us would take a breather by sitting on the floor and catching up on our drinking.

Sometime after 1:30, the novelty of playing hockey with brooms and produce in the kitchen waned. Mr. B grabbed the last orange and blew past The Big Man, faking him out of his shorts, firing the orb through a mostly drunk Douglas and into the hallway. He danced around on the slippery floor, pointing and taunting The Big Man, lying flat on his ass in the middle of the kitchen.

He enthusiastically leaped over the prone Douglas to retrieve the orange that came to rest in the hallway. As Mr. B reached down, The Big Man, who had about enough of the taunting, tackled him from behind like he was sacking the quarterback, driving him face-first into the carpet. The vibration resonated all the way to Massapequa.

With the total weight of The Big Man still on his back, Mr. B wiggled out from under him. He groggily struggled while rising upright onto his feet, only to have his knees buckle, so he sat back down Indian style.

That's when we spotted the bleeding cut over his left eyebrow. Being violently driven into a rug face first will do that.

We helped the pale-looking Mr. B on his feet and onto one of the relocated kitchen chairs. We didn't know much about concussion protocol back then, but I bet Mr. B got his bell rung.

Running back into the kitchen, I wet a dish towel, using it to help stop the blood from flowing. The Big Man grabbed another towel and wrapped ice cubes inside. Douglas opened the fridge and picked out a few beers.

"This doesn't look good," I told The Big Man as I wiped more blood off Mr. B's forehead.

"He'll be fine," said Douglas, cracking open another tall boy.

Mr. B kept one eye closed like a pirate. "This fucking hurts."

With a flap of skin hanging on by a thread over Mr. B's left eye, blood began trickling down his face at an alarming rate. I gave Mr. B the towel filled with ice and told him to keep it pressed against his head so the pressure would stop the bleeding. He resembled a crime victim with his primarily white T-shirt now sporting excess blood. Perhaps he was.

The ice kept the swelling down, so things started looking up. But Mr. B was curious about what he looked like, which we highly discouraged. He defiantly wobbled to his feet and headed for the bathroom right off the kitchen. We waited patiently for the expected cry of "Holy Fuck!" and were not disappointed.

The precipitation morphed into freezing rain. The fluffy snow from this morning glistened like a sheet of ice, stretching along the path from the front door to the driveway. I thought about suggesting we head outside and continue the game if the rain ended when I saw something that scared the daylights out of me.

Cars were carefully pulling into the icy driveway.

CHAPTER 5
THE CRIME SCENE

"They're fucking home!" I shouted to no one in particular.

All seven of our working eyeballs were now staring out the giant windows, watching in horror as the cars settled into the driveway. We stared in silence as they carefully emerged from the vehicles, having to grab onto the car doors and each other to not fall on the slippery surface covering the walkway.

Seeing them slipping and sliding snapped us out of our fear-induced petrification. We had just a few minutes while they negotiated the icy trail before they reached the door and entered the middle of a crime scene.

Mr. B retreated with the bloody towel to the girl's bedroom while we sprang into action. Big Man and I quickly returned the dinette table and chairs to the kitchen. With a cat's quickness, Douglas swept the floor free of the straw remnants and broken fruit to a reasonable degree.

I kept an eye on the approaching populous. Negotiating the icy incline from the driveway to the front steps was more treacherous than I initially thought. However, it bought us a precious few additional minutes.

We restored the kitchen to its original configuration except for the fruit bowl's contents. A garbage pail of dead fruit left us nothing to return to the bowl. Maybe they would think we were eating healthy.

Douglas returned the brooms to the closet, albeit several bristles lighter than when the morning started, when the door opened, and the rest of our weekend companions stepped inside.

The Dower sisters and Kerri were the first in and shouted as a warning, "We're back!" Curiously, we weren't playing pool, and the stereo was off. To this day, bless their little hearts, they knew we were most likely up to something and hoped they could provide us a 30-

second window to stop whatever we were doing and prepare for the adults returning.

They rushed up the stairs to find three of us sitting on comfy chairs in the dining room area, quietly nursing beers and conversing casually.

"What are you guys doing?" Kerri asked.

Douglas looked up at Kerri from the magazine he was pretending to read, reached for his beer, and took a quick sip. "Us? Why, we're just relaxing and enjoying an adult beverage. What does it look like we're doing?"

"Bullshit," said Barbara, who would one day become an inspector in the Nassau County Police Department.

She eyeballed us, noticing we were sweating like pigs. Also, there was an overwhelming odor of oranges emanating from the kitchen.

Kerri pointed to the red spot where Bruce's head landed on the carpet. "What the fuck is that?"

Our 30-second window quickly expired as the rest of the skiing party made their way through the door.

Barbara glanced around and leaned closer to us, "Where's Bruce?"

The jig was up.

I sheepishly pointed to the closed bedroom door, and they rushed inside, making sure to close the door behind them. While the others stripped off their winter gear in the playroom downstairs, you could easily hear the voices inside the bedroom.

"What the fuck happened to you!"

"You're bleeding!"

"You have to go to the hospital!"

Now the jig was really up.

"What's going on up there?" Russ Dower called from downstairs. "Jesus H. Christ, what happened now?"

He hurried up the stairs and found the three of us trying to act innocent while being guilty. "What the hell is going on?" Without waiting for an answer, he headed to the girl's room to see for himself, opened the door, and looked inside.

"Oh, jeez," he said.

With the rest of the group ascending the stairs, Doug's mother, Eileen, looked our way and asked her son directly, "What happened?"

Never one to lie to his mother, Douglas explained we were playfully wrestling when Bruce fell and scraped his head on the rug.

Russ then emerged with the girls and Bruce, holding a bloodstained dishtowel above his left eye.

"He has to go to a hospital and get this stitched."

"Oh, my God!" exclaimed Eileen.

"What the hell were you assholes doing?" Mr. Finkernagle asked.

We sprang to action, and Douglas said, "We'll take him now."

Surprisingly, no one objected. The fact that none of us should have been allowed to operate a vehicle, let alone in icy conditions, was irrelevant.

While the girls were playing mother hen and fawning over Mr. B like a damaged movie star, we found our coats and suited up for the drive to the emergency room at Lehigh Valley Hospital, a few miles north of I-80.

As the last one to exit, I reached for the handle to close the door and heard a voice from the kitchen, "Hey, what happened to all the fruit?"

CHAPTER 6
THE EMERGENCY ROOM

Under the guidance of the designated navigator, Douglas, Big Man deftly maneuvered the Catalina with caution through the icy local roads and onto the newly sanded surfaces of I-80. The usual 20-minute trip to the ER took twice as long while the wintery mix fell lightly. We didn't arrive until nearly 3:00 in the afternoon.

Somehow, Douglas snatched the now half-empty bottle of Jack from the kitchen. We passed it around like a group of bums sitting under a bridge, each taking a few swigs before heading inside.

The ER was quiet, and Mr. B was seen quickly. Soon, Douglas was maneuvering around the waiting room, inviting everyone he met to the party later that evening at our little chalet in the Pocono mountains. He asked almost every female member we met, but most politely declined because they would be working all night. He secured a few maybes and one reply of "sounds good."

Fortunately for us, or unfortunately, we spent only 30 minutes there. Mr. B emerged from the treatment area with his red and white wool hat pulled over his injured forehead.

"No stitches," he announced, pulling off his hat like a magician and exposing a funny-looking bandage over his left eye. "There was nothing to stitch. They just put a butterfly bandage on it and told me to keep it clean."

"What do we do now?" I asked.

"Time to celebrate," said Douglas. "Let's find a liquor store and pick up some vodka and gin for tonight's festivities."

The sleet and freezing rain stopped, and things were looking up with the sun breaking through.

Douglas asked the security guard where we might find a liquor store, and he suggested we head to Main Street. We were already in the college town of East Stroudsburg.

"There's a good chance you'll find one there," he said with a wink.

Of course, he was right.

A vast, two-lane thoroughfare, Main Street's parking configuration opted for diagonal spaces instead of the traditional ones spaced parallel to the curb, making it much easier to pull in than out of. We spotted a liquor store with an open spot directly in front.

Douglas, grinning like a kid in a candy store, exited the car before The Big Man had even put it into park. "I got this."

I decided to follow behind him anyway.

Inside, he procured bottles of vodka and gin and handed them to me to hold like a supermarket basket. I obediently balanced one in each hand and headed to the register. Doug picked up some Jack to replace the one we found earlier in the kitchen cabinet and had just finished.

Once at the register, I reached into my pocket for cash, and Douglas waved me off.

"Nonsense."

Paying the clerk, he spied a bottle of grain alcohol (120 proof) on the counter. Grabbing the quart-sized container of the clear liquid, Douglas held it to the light as if examining a fine wine. "Wait. Wrap this up, too."

Turning to me, he asked, "You ever drink grain alcohol?"

I shook my head negatively.

"Oh, you're in for a treat."

We returned to the car with our booty, and Douglas displayed the grain alcohol, presenting it like the Holy Grail.

"Before we go anywhere, shall we have a taste?"

The Big Man looked puzzled. "What the fuck is that?"

Sounding like an expert, I told him it was 120-proof grain alcohol.

Douglas broke the seal on the skinny neck, removed the cap, and took a swig. We watched in horror as his face recoiled like he swallowed sewer water.

Shrugging his head back and forth, he handed it to me. "Wow, what a kick!"

As horrified as I might have been, what choice did I have?

I grabbed it and took a sniff. For all I knew, the odorless bottle could have been filled with tap water. Moving the bottleneck to my lips, I spied a Cheshire Cat-grinning Douglas, meaning one of two things. Either he knew something I didn't know, or, being utterly wasted, he could only manage a smile at the time.

He knew something I didn't know but would find out fairly quickly.

CHAPTER 7
THE VILLAGE PUB

Instead of being cautious and taking a tiny sip, I leaned into the bottle of grain alcohol and took a bravado-induced healthy swig.

At first, I thought I swallowed firewater. The burning sensation in my throat felt like nothing I had ever experienced, including downing a few flaming shots of Yukon Jack. When I finally opened my eyes after recoiling, I saw Douglas beginning to laugh. "Good, right?"

I recovered enough to croak out, "That was the worst thing I have ever tasted."

A defiant Mr. B grabbed it from my shaking hand before I could put the cap back on. "Gimme that."

Bending his head back and putting the bottle to his mouth, we could see an air bubble rise from the inverted neck as he took a big sip.

His silence was deafening.

Douglas continued to giggle uncontrollably.

After an unusually long pause, Mr. B whispered a gravelly, "What the fuck?"

With Mr. B shoving the bottle in front of his face, The Big Man shook his head. "No thanks."

Instead, he pointed across the street to a pair of neon signs for Budweiser and Heineken in the window of The Village Pub. "I could use a drink, but not that shit."

With my intestinal tract still on fire, I joined the slightly inebriated trio, and we headed across the street. The brief sunshine was slowly overtaken by cloud cover, and with darkness approaching, there was still a little light left in the day.

Located in the college town of the East Stroudsburg University Warriors, The Village Pub resembled your basic dive bar. We hoped for a crowd of beautiful co-eds happily drinking on a Saturday, looking for a party later that night. Instead, with ESU students on Winter

Break, our presence inside The Village Pub only doubled the late afternoon occupancy.

The bar extended halfway down the right side against the wall with an open back area containing a pool table and the bathrooms. The three other patrons peeked up from their drinks while a song from Aerosmith played on the jukebox. In anticipation of the Super Bowl tomorrow, the black and yellow colors of the Steelers dominated the available wall space.

"Go, Steelers!" I said as we walked in, pumping my fist for emphasis. Although the locals initially met us with a friendly wave, something gave us away as interlopers.

The smile disappeared from the bartender's face. "Are you guys from New York?"

"Yep," I said, suddenly remembering the Mets hat on my head, "But we're out here skiing and rooting for the yellow and black!"

This affirmation appeased the regulars, and we took our place at the far end of the bar, near the pool table.

We intended to have a quick drink, head back to the house for dinner, and set up for the party. Douglas extended invitations to the other "day" drinkers and the bartender. Checking out the décor, we noticed writing on the suspended ceiling above our heads. After further inspection, the scribblings covered most of the panels.

The bartender informed us that visitors have inscribed their names on the ceiling for years. It's kind of a calling card for the pub. He tossed us a sharpie and invited us to find a spot and join the tradition. I found a small, blank area on a ceiling tile near the bathrooms. Grabbing a stool, I reached up to inscribe, "Team FUBAR was here January 20, 1979."

After three or four drinks and a few games of pool, Mr. B noticed darkness had overtaken the initial twilight outside during our unexpected sojourn to The Village Pub. In addition, it had been snowing and accumulating on the street and the cars.

"What time is it?" Mr. B asked after glancing out the window. Gotta be close to 5:00, right?"

I checked my watch. We passed 5:00 more than an hour ago.

"It's almost 6:30," I said.

"Oh, shit," Douglas commented. "Dinner was at 6:00."

The Big Man was leaning over the pool table with one eye open as he lined up the red-striped eleven ball to bang it across the beer-stained green felt and into the far pocket. "Well, I suggest we finish these drinks and vamoose, no?"

"Nonsense, Gregory," said Douglas, signaling the bartender for another round, "One more, my friend!"

Crawling out of the Village Pub and into the now heavily falling snow, we were shitfaced. Darkness had a secure hold on the evening, although the light reflecting from the streetlights on the snowy surfaces was an added plus.

Douglas volunteered to drive because he touted his knowledge of the area and ability to get us back to the chalet. In retrospect, that might not have been the best decision, but it seemed like a good idea at the time.

Being his father's car, The Big Man sat shotgun while Mr. B and I were in the back. I settled behind Douglas, who seemed to be in complete control of the Catalina as we slid through the snow on Main Street and onto Route 80.

Driving with limited visibility in the raging snowstorm, Douglas cruised on I-80, passing cars and trucks with alarming frequency. He was maneuvering the Catalina like an Italian sports car being chased by the paparazzi.

During the 40-minute trip, I could feel death's breath on the back of my neck. I kept one eye open, hoping to recognize death when it finally came. I remember The Big Man yelling things like, "Watch out!" and "Are you kidding me?" as Douglas stayed laser-focused on the windshield and laughed maniacally. If I had to guess, a passed-out Mr. B had no idea of our impending doom. But when I looked in his direction, I could see the panic was also frozen on his face.

CHAPTER 8
THE CONFRONTATION

I recited a small, private prayer when we exited Route 80. We cheated death more than once, and it was just a matter of time as we snaked our way through the local roads to the chalet.

The fluffy snow made the drive safer on the local road surfaces. When we arrived at the house, the previously icy driveway was now blanketed with fresh powder. The new crunchy surface let us quickly make our way up the incline to the front door. It looked like someone took the time to spread sand or salt on the pavement.

"You think they'll be mad?" Mr. B inquired as we approached the front door.

"Nonsense," said Douglas, "So we missed dinner. What's the big deal?"

"Yeah," said The Big Man, concocting a quick cover story, "Let's just tell them we were in the ER for a long time."

Before we could open the door, Barbara and Kerri beat us to it and simultaneously yelled, "Where the fuck were you guys?"

We didn't even have a chance to breathe.

"Why didn't you call us?" said Kerri, "We've been worried sick. We called the hospital, and they said you left hours ago."

So much for our solid-as-a-rock cover story.

After shedding our winter gear, we ambled upstairs, and Bruce explained what had happened at the ER, showing off his battle scar. We fessed up to imbibing with a drink or two at the local bar, but nobody was buying those calculations. We were obviously wasted and should never have been driving. At this point, trying to make an excuse for being over two hours late for dinner would have been a waste of time.

Mr. and Mrs. Dower were having none of it and immediately

berated Douglas. If any of our parents were on this trip, we certainly would have been the primary targets.

Soon, the four of us were being stared at as if we were holding bloody knives at a murder scene. Unfortunately, finding a hole to crawl into would be difficult.

With insults and admonishments surrounding us like gnats, we got a little pissed off and defensive. After all, we didn't hurt anyone; we just missed dinner. Well, we hurt Mr. B, but that's beside the point. They were treating us like pariahs, which wasn't fair in our eyes.

Placing our tails between our legs, we walked to the kitchen and grabbed a few plates from the cupboard. The adults had been enjoying themselves as the bottles of vodka and gin were down to the last drops. I noted one bottle of scotch had been drained while the other was down about a pint.

After surveying the room, we found Russ and Mr. Finkernagle had been hitting it pretty hard. They were in no position to comment on our obvious inebriation, considering it had been almost an hour since our last drink.

Looking for something to eat, we walked into the kitchen. From his comfy chair in the sitting room, Mr. Finkernagle commented, "I guess you assholes expect something to eat, right?"

Whoa.

Who the fuck is this guy to call us assholes?

It's one thing to be called assholes by the Dowers because we would have deserved it. But this Hammerhead? How dare he comment at all.

I looked at Mr. B and saw smoke coming from his ears.

"Fuck this," he said. "Let's get the fuck out of here."

"You're right," Douglas said. "This is bullshit."

To join in with the crowd, I agreed. We didn't deserve treatment like this.

The three of us exited the dining room table without eating anything. The Big Man snagged a chicken leg and said, "Can't we eat before we go?"

The snow continued falling as we packed our bags and dismantled the stereo. Barbara, Kerri, and Mrs. Dower were pleading with us to reconsider. Susan pulled Big Man to the side. They dated a few times, but their romantic relationship didn't seem to go anywhere. The Big Man secretly hoped to find a way to end it without much fanfare.

"You *are* an asshole, you know," Susan told him.

"I know," said a smiling Big Man, aware his status had now changed from being 'in a relationship' to being a 'friend.'

With our bags packed and the stereo equipment disassembled, we started loading everything into the car, which took a few trips. Each time we returned inside, the girls pleaded with us to reconsider and stay the night, then leave tomorrow morning.

The more they pleaded with us, the more indignant we got.

"That guy called us assholes," said Mr. B. "I'm not staying here."

"Fuck him," I said, waving at the upper level. Although the thought of driving back to Massapequa in a snowstorm at this time of night was a bit of a concern, I wasn't going to suggest we reconsider. I deserved the moniker of an asshole as much as anyone in our little group.

"This is so stupid," Barbara said, tears in her eyes. "Please don't go!"

But we had already committed, and turning back now would brand us as pussies for the rest of our lives. Well, maybe that's a slight exaggeration. After all, crawling from the wreckage of a fiery crash or plunging over the side of the George Washington Bridge in a snowstorm hardly qualified as a reason to erect a statue in our honor.

We finished loading the car and returned to say our last goodbyes. The girls, including Mrs. Dower, watched forlornly from the open front door as we pulled away as if they would never see us again.

If anything, I knew we would never see the Finkernagles again.

CHAPTER 9
THE PROBLEMS WITH THE CATALINA

It continued snowing hard as we approached Route 80 East, heading out of Pennsylvania, across the Delaware Water Gap, and into New Jersey. I rode shotgun while Mr. B and Douglas took to the backseat. Knowing The Big Man's dislike for driving at night, I offered to take over.

Pulling over to the shoulder, we changed places.

It didn't take long for him to begin dozing in the navigator seat. With Douglas already gone, Mr. B kept me company from behind. The drive home went smoothly until we got a few miles from the George Washington Bridge. I detected the interior lights dimming and the radio volume slowly decreasing.

I thought nothing of it as we approached the brightly lit toll plaza. I grabbed some cash from my money clip and paid the toll. By the time we hit the middle of the bridge and were in darkness again, I was sure the dashboard lights were not only dimming but were virtually nonexistent.

I looked for Mr. B in the rearview mirror and saw him sleeping peacefully. Leaving me no choice, I poked The Big Man awake to inform him of our current situation. The headlights were still on, but they weren't very effective. Something was happening with the electrical system. Even the radio stopped working.

"I think we have a problem with the electrical system."

The Big Man slowly opened one eye to see who was poking the bear, then closed it again. "Is the engine still running?"

"So far," I said.

"Then let's not worry about it for now," he said before settling back into his seat and heading back to La-La-Land.

I guess he was right. What were we going to do about it anyway?

Besides Douglas, who was long gone, none of us knew anything about cars or electrical systems, so stopping and opening the hood would be fruitless. Considering we didn't know the Las Vegas odds of the car starting again, stopping the vehicle for any reason might not have been a good idea.

With three sleeping giants, no radio to listen to, and a darkened interior, I fought the urge to close my eyes and tried to stay awake. I decided to open the window and get some fresh air. Listening to music inside my head, we escaped New Jersey and zipped through the Bronx. Negotiating the potholes on the Cross Bronx Expressway helped me focus on driving. I soldiered over the Throgs Neck Bridge and down the Cross Island Parkway toward Long Island, eventually landing on the Southern State Parkway.

Somewhere around Meadowbrook Parkway, about six miles from Massapequa, the car started shimmying like we had a flat tire, only we weren't listing to one side. I could hear a loud, vibrating sound from outside the open driver's side window. I poked The Big Man awake again and asked him about the noise. Of course, he had no idea.

All he could manage was a mumble. "Sounds like a flat tire."

I drove on many bad tires during my young adult life and knew a flat immediately caused the car to pull to that side. Instead of a vibrating sound, this was more of a flapping sound.

"It's not flat."

"Is the car still running?"

"So far."

"Then let's not worry about it until we have to."

I closed the window to quiet the sound, but the vibration woke Mr. B.

"What the hell is that?" he asked.

"We're not sure," I informed him, "But we can still drive with it, so we got that going for us."

As I slowed down on the exit ramp for Broadway in Massapequa, the vibration also diminished to a low hum.

"Maybe we have some snow caught in the wheel well?" I suggested. Mr. B agreed with my hypothesis, and we continued to Doug's house, just south of Merrick Road, vibrating car and all.

It was after 1:00, and we decided to take Douglas's suggestion to crash at his house to watch the Super Bowl tomorrow. We had our sleeping bags and were in no shape to argue. None of us wanted to unload the Catalina at this hour and trudge to our parent's houses.

We left the wounded Catalina in the driveway and headed inside, settling on the living room furniture. The Big Man took the couch, I curled up on the loveseat, and Mr. B passed out on the floor. With the disaster of the skiing trip in our rearview mirror, we didn't even wake until we heard Douglas in the kitchen making breakfast.

Again.

CHAPTER 10
THE AFTERMATH

It was almost noon when we made our way to the kitchen. Curiously, a fruit basket sat on the table. The Big Man playfully picked up an orange and was about to fire it at Douglas when I seized his arm and said, "Don't you dare...."

Unaware of how close we came to a reenactment of the Pennsylvania kitchen debacle 24 hours ago, Douglas once again displayed his culinary skills and prepared a great breakfast. He had been up for about an hour and went to the store to pick up some beer and munch items. After all, watching the Super Bowl would require supplies, correct?

After eating, we settled into the comforts of the living room, but except for Douglas, we weren't in a beer-drinking mood. He brought a round of beers for everyone, which he eagerly opened. However, we were having no part of grain alcohol again. I tried my best to enjoy the beer but felt too far gone. I noticed The Big Man and Mr. B also had problems imbibing and keeping up with Douglas. When offering to make a trip to the kitchen for more beer. He had no takers.

"What are you guys, lightweights?" he asked. "It's the fucking Super Bowl, for Christ's sake!"

Douglas could be very persuasive.

I took another but had to nurse it while we watched the game. Approaching half-time, I was shot. The weekend events caught up to me, and I couldn't drink anymore. I just wanted to go home. Just then, as if on cue, someone was opening the front door.

It was the Dowers.

Apparently, they didn't stay in the Poconos for the game either. I often wonder if the events from the previous evening contributed to their early exit.

Douglas raced to the door to intercept his parents, leaving us trapped in the living room. We knew this wouldn't end well when we heard muffled arguing from the hallway. Barbara, Susan, and Kerri approached us while Douglas continued his discussion with Eileen and Russ.

"I'm glad you guys are okay," Barbara said as we hugged. Susan didn't hug The Big Man, but that was to be expected.

There were no two ways about it; we were directly responsible for the disaster in Pennsylvania.

We took the hint and gathered our stuff. Making our way toward the front door, Mrs. Dower appeared happy to see us, but Mr. Dower was just as delighted to see us go. We thanked them for everything and apologized for what happened at the chalet. What more could we say?

Looking at the Catalina in daylight for the first time, The Big Man noticed the front tire on the driver's side stripped entirely of rubber. We had been riding on the steel belted radial. The tire on the passenger side was also tearing, with the rubber flapping in the breeze.

"Looks like I'm going to have to get new tires."

"Don't forget about the lights," I reminded him.

"What lights?"

He hadn't even registered that all the interior lights and the radio were no longer working. He shook his head. "My father's gonna kick my ass…"

We cleared the last of the snow off the car's windshield and got inside. The Big Man smiled at me before turning the ignition key. "Here goes nothing."

The engine sputtered to life, and we were on our way, balding, vibrating tires and all.

PART THREE

AND SO IT GOES

The Excommunication of Jeff Luft

(February 1979)

CHAPTER 1
THE SETUP

Sometimes, working for a college newspaper has its advantages. The Long Island bar scene in the late '70s was huge.

Your Humble Narrator

My friend Bruce (Mr. B) and I collaborated on a weekly column, Brewing Out, which reviewed local bars we visited during the weekend. Our tales of debauchery provided a service to the student body and many laughs along the way.

Written under the pseudonym of Team FUBAR (Fucked Up Beyond All Repair) allowed us to visit taverns anonymously and report to our readers about the three B's–Beers, Bucks, and Babes. To our fellow students of New York Tech, we were gods. We spoke their language. Brewing Out was very popular, leaving everyone wondering who these wild and crazy guys from Team FUBAR were.

Students began to inquire as to how they could join Team FUBAR. Of course, the aura surrounding Team FUBAR was our secret identity. To the kids who read our column, we were only known as Disco, Mr. B, The Catman (my cousin Sal), and Eggy (our friend enrolled at Hofstra). Although outsiders could never become actual members of The Team, we invented a membership level to allow them to participate in some festivities.

To obtain the status of "MIGS" (Member in Good Standing), applicants submitted an application touting their credentials for consideration. Some were way, way out there, even by our standards. Unfortunately for us, they were primarily males.

Some of our colleagues on the New York Institute of Technology student newspaper, *The Campus Slate*, became interested in achieving MIGS status, including one of the newer guys, Jeff Luft. He was a tall, skinny white guy with an afro and a gift for gab, complimented with Balls of Steel. Luft had a knack for arranging interviews with big-name musicians and performers in movies and TV. Without fear of rejection, he would cold-call talent agencies and record labels until he connected with someone to authorize an interview.

We got along well, and he was pleasant most of the time, but he wanted to be recognized as a MIGS.

One afternoon, while working on my sports column in *The Slate's* underground office, he approached my desk to chat. He grabbed an old, musty-smelling side chair and positioned himself to my right. "What do I have to do to become a MIGS?"

For Jeff to be worthy of such an honor, I explained he must prove he is an outstanding party animal (which he wasn't).

"What if I could get you guys an interview with Southside Johnny?" he said with a smile, knowing Bruce and I were enormous fans.

"That, my friend, would get you a seat at the table."

Reaching into his jacket, he pulled out a small spiral notepad. Flipping through the pages, he paused in the middle, grabbed the receiver of the black phone on my desk, crossed his legs like a 1950s secretary, and began dialing. I stopped typing to better listen to his end of the conversation.

After identifying himself and requesting to speak to a specific individual, he waited patiently for the connection, arching his eyebrows and looking at me to ensure I was paying attention. Once he engaged with the other party, he sounded so professional that nobody would believe he was just this kid from a stupid commuter college.

"Okay, Okay," he said, scribbling notes on his little pad. "Yes, we can make that work."

This was starting to get interesting.

Luft's voice was confident. "Sure, I know where that is. Yes, next Sunday, February 18th, at 6:00 pm. Yes. Yes. We have two reporters and a photographer."

A photographer?

"Thank you so much," he continued. "Yes, of course I will. Have a great day!"

As he hung up the phone, he supported a Cheshire Cat-sized grin. "You're in! We have an interview with Southside Johnny next Sunday at some place called The Factory in Staten Island. There's a show at 8:00, and we can talk to him around 6:00. I'll go with you and take pictures."

I was so happy I could have kissed him on the lips, but I didn't. Instead, I made him an honorary MIGS right on the spot.

THE CAMPUS SLATE PRESENTS:

Team F.U.B.A.R.'s

Team F.U.B.A.R. is a group of four students who are Fouled Up Beyond All Repair and write Brewing Out. We are looking for charter members who are into the same things that we write about, Drinking and ~~sex~~(only kidding). But seriously, we want to meet the other people who are into drinking beer, ~~xx~~ and this is the only way. If you feel that you could be a member of Team F.U.B.A.R., drop this appication in our Mail Box in the Dairy Barn, the Slate Office, or an official Team F.U.B.A.R. envelope located around campus. Also, if you know of someone who you think could qualify as F.U.B.A.R.ite of the Year, write his/her name and a breif reason why. The F.U.B.A.R.X Xite of the Year will be honored in the 2/7 column of Brewing Out. Remember, print or use crayon, we are just as toasted as you and neatness counts. We are working twoards a Team F.U.B.A.R. night at the Pub, but we need your help. Join Team F.U.B.A.R. and burn with us. Thanks, Team F.U.B.A.R.

(Just a bunch of crazy guys)

Check One

X CHARTER MEMBER   ___ F.U.B.A.R.ITE OF YEAR

Peter A. ███████

I want to become a charter member because I am fried. Need more be said?

Say no more, say no more.

CHAPTER 2
THE STONY OPEN (IV)

Mr. B's eyes lit up. "Are you fucking with me?"

"No, I'm serious. Fucking Luft arranged the whole thing. I was sitting right there listening in!"

The Jukes released their third album, *Hearts of Stone*, in October of 1978, and it became one of our favorites. Seeing them perform was great, but this was something different. Mr. B and I were going to sit down and talk to him.

Using a Rand McNally road map for navigation like Magellan, we found The Factory off Seguine Avenue on Johnston Terrace, down by the water in the Princess Bay section of Staten Island. It was about 20 miles from the Verrazano Bridge off Hylan Boulevard, quite a trek from Massapequa.

"Wait," Bruce said. "Did you say next Sunday?"

"Yeah, why?"

"Aren't we going out to Stony Brook on Saturday for the Tech game?"

New York Tech was playing Stony Brook in basketball, and we planned a road trip to meet with friends who were students there and lived in an on-campus dorm. The sheer amount of booze, smoking, and debauchery in previous visits allowed us to dub these extravaganzas "Stony Opens." To mark them for the history books, this one would be "Stony Open IV."

"How bad could it be?" I asked, knowing full well how bad it could be. "We don't have to be in Staten Island until 6:00 pm the next day."

Except for The Big Man, who was in California on vacation, we assembled the usual lineup of crazies for the Stony Brook trip, including my younger brother Tony, Barbara Dower, her brother Douglas, and their friend Kerri Barr. Saturday was shaping up as a blowout.

After hearing about a Southside Johnny show in Staten Island scheduled for the next day, everyone was gung-ho for an entire weekend of destruction.

During the week, Mr. B and I conferred with our friends to compile a list of questions to ask. Douglas suggested we find out why he doesn't have a driver's license and what kind of beer he likes. Kerri and Barbara read somewhere he doesn't enjoy discussing his relationship with Bruce Springsteen, so we should avoid that subject at all costs.

Searching through my parent's junk drawer, I secured a fresh set of C-sized batteries for my portable cassette recorder to ensure I didn't miss anything. I made sure to pack my trusty reporter's flip pad and two black Flair markers. During the days leading up to the interview, I filled a few pages in my notepad with questions I wanted to ask. I was ready.

Of course, Saturday at Stony Brook was off the charts. After a full day of drinking and partying, we attended the basketball game (NY Tech lost). Once I completed some player interviews for my game story, I caught up with everyone in one of the dorms. Before the night was over, we would journey to three different bars.

After spending a disappointing hour at The Mad Hatter (which included a wasted two-dollar cover charge), we cruised to The Pubbery. At least at The Mad Hatter, the bartender knew how to make an Alabama Slammer. The dudes at the Pubbery needed to be educated. Once inside, Douglas collected quarters from everyone to feed the jukebox, becoming the unofficial DJ. Sometime around 2:00 am, we left and picked up a few beers across the street at the 7-11.

With the witching hour of last call for alcohol rapidly approaching, we made our way to The Hayloft for what we thought would be our final stop of the evening. Although disco music was still blasting, most of the dancing fools had already vacated the premises by this late hour. Douglas convinced the DJ to put on rock and roll for the remaining diehards.

Mr. B and Kerri decided to have some fun with the stragglers, pretending to have a heated discussion about abortion.

"You have GOT to have the abortion," Mr. B yelled. "Don't worry. I'll pay for it!"

"But it's my baby!" Kerri answered back, "And I don't want an abortion!"

"I don't care," Mr. B said, turning up the volume as the onlookers stared in horror, "You have got to have an abortion…."

You get the drift…

Last call in New York State was at 4:00 am, but we were already an hour past that deadline. Once the bartender announced last call, the remaining 15 or so people in the bar started chanting, "Con-doh," which was the terminology back then for Condominium. Some random guy invited everyone back to his condo out east for an after-hours party. As toasted as we were, we unthinkingly followed the caravan to an unknown location.

On the way, Barbara must have accidentally cut off some asshole's Cadillac. He was ranting and raving, waving his arm out the window and driving erratically. I noticed what was going on and immediately pulled next to him. He promptly gave me the finger, so I did what any true friend would do to protect the women they loved. I nudged him off the road.

He chased after us to the parking lot of the guy's condo. Exiting our cars, we milled about when he approached us with his car. My brother Tony gave the side of his vehicle a massive kick with his hunting boot, leaving a deep dent and resulting in him peeling out. We never saw him again.

As trashed as we were, we made an executive decision to forgo the impromptu party at this stranger's condo and headed home.

When we arrived home, it was after sunrise. We had to be in Staten Island in less than 12 hours.

CHAPTER 3
THE FACTORY

I woke up around 1:00 on Sunday and started making phone calls. Unlike everyone's gun-ho attitude of the previous night, nobody I called would commit to making the trip with us to Staten Island other than my brother.

Although everyone was on board while partying at Stony Brook the previous night, only Barbara and Kerri would even "try" to make it. To be honest, if it weren't for the opportunity to interview Southside Johnny, I would have bailed myself. Besides, the weatherman indicated a chance of some snow overnight. I wasn't looking forward to driving home from Staten Island after a Jukes concert in normal conditions, let alone a possible snowstorm.

That said, the blizzard threat wouldn't stop me because I had a master plan. My girlfriend Lisa had an apartment in Baldwin, and I invited her to come along for a few reasons. Number one, she was a massive fan of Southside Johnny. Number two, it was vital that she be an eyewitness to exactly how cool her boyfriend was, getting to interview Southside. Number three, I would try to spend the night with her.

Mr. B, my brother Tony, Lisa, and I were going to pick up Luft and drive to Staten Island in Tony's car, the Beast of Burden, but I had other ideas. Instead, I wanted them to follow me to Baldwin, where I would leave my car. Upon returning from Staten Island, they would drop us off in Baldwin, and I would administer a proper goodbye (wink, wink).

A good plan, right?

It would be a long trip to Staten Island, so we packed a cooler full of beer and some snacks for the ride. Plus, we would have at least an hour to kill between the interview and the Jukes concert. Mr. B and I rolled a few doobies for the evening and, along with Tony, set out on our adventure.

Tony and Mr. B picked up Luft on the way to Baldwin, where Lisa and I were waiting. Cracking open a couple of beers and firing up one of the joints, we got comfortable in The Beast and headed to Staten Island at about 3:00.

Once over the Verrazano Bridge, we traveled to the far reaches of Staten Island before finding the exit for Hylan Boulevard. Making a left on Seguine Ave and past the hospital, we joked about hoping we didn't end up there at some point in the evening.

A nondescript white building down a dead-end street near the docks bore blood-red letters spelling out "The Factory." A light blue tour bus with white and red racing stripes idled in the far reaches of the parking lot. After maneuvering closer to the building, we tentatively stepped inside even though it didn't look open yet.

The Factory didn't have assigned seating, so we didn't need tickets, only to pay the $6.00 cover charge and get our hands stamped. Once inside, a small gathering space separated the entrance from the larger room. Here, we found two pinball games, some tall bistro tables (no chairs), and a bathroom for each gender. At the far end, a king-sized square bar led into the concert hall area, which contained a stage and dance floor.

The hall was cavernous, and without people, it provided a creepy echo when you talked. The stools surrounding the bar were the only seating available. The bar was conveniently located between the concert and gathering areas.

When we arrived at 5:30, only a handful of people, including a bartender, were inside, so we grabbed spots at the bar and ordered a couple of beers. After peeling off our coats (it was February, after all), we draped them over a few empty stools since The Factory did not have a coat check.

"So, what do we do now?" I asked Luft, who looked the other way as if searching for someone. "Are you sure we're getting on that bus?"

"I talked to the manager to confirm before you guys picked me up," he said, getting off his stool and walking toward the front door. "I'm gonna go to the bus and see what's happening."

Mr. B reached out and grabbed him by the arm. "You better be sure we get on that bus, or I'm going to kick your ass all over Staten Island."

Luft approached the door and started a conversation with someone entering the building. After a few minutes, they waved us over.

We quaffed the remaining beer in our bottles and gathered our coats. Strangely, the others also began stirring and putting on their coats. They followed us out the door and into the parking lot as we walked toward the tour bus.

Enquiring minds want to know, so I tapped Luft on his arm and pointed over my right shoulder with my thumb. "What's going on, Buddy?"

"They're from Hofstra and some college in New Jersey," he said. "They'll be interviewing at the same time. It's a group interview."

"That's bullshit," I said. "When did that happen?"

Luft explained group interviews are done all the time with college students. Funny, but I didn't recall any mention of a group interview.

Well, beggars can't be choosers. This was starting to sound like a news conference instead of an interview.

In my best imitation of Moe from the Three Stooges, I turned to Mr. B, pointed to Luft, and said, "Remind me to kill him later."

CHAPTER 4
THE INTERVIEW

Approaching the bus, we let the chick from Hofstra board first (we are gentlemen, after all) and followed behind for a better look at her ass. As the procession made its way to the back, we politely waived to some of the crew and band members, who were comfortably hanging out on couches and chairs watching a movie on the small TV.

In the back section, Southside Johnny sat at a corner table wearing his trademark sunglasses, a red T-shirt with a white Factory logo, and a grey velour hoodie zipped halfway up. Seating areas lined both sidewalls, so we all settled in and began introducing ourselves and what school we represented. Southside was polite, engaging, and very funny.

Unsure of the proper procedure for asking questions in a group setting, we didn't want to act like fanboys and fawn all over him. And we certainly didn't want to ask anything about Springsteen.

"So," Southside said, looking directly at the cute chick from Hofstra (not that we could blame him), "Fire away. What do ya want to know?"

She smiled and launched into her first question, "How close are you with Bruce Springsteen? Are you personal friends or just business friends?"

Jesus H. Christ...

The interview went well, I thought. After answering fluff questions from the others, we took over and got Southside to dish on several topics not usually broached in a Q&A session. Using questions from my notes compiled during those foggy nights at Jocelyn's, he confirmed never receiving a driver's license and hated record company executives. He'd rather listen to a bar band playing R&B than a band like Yes perform in concert.

Southside laughed long and loud when we told him we authored a weekly drinking column reviewing Long Island bars. When asked about his favorite beer, he grinned and said, "What d'ya got?" Later, he admitted to liking Miller and hating Heineken. When asked if he had a message for his fans about the new album, *Hearts of Stone*, he calmly said, "If they don't buy the album, I'll kill them."

The South recited many stories, leaving us to believe this was the type of guy we'd like to knock down a few with.

While the others began to file out of the back area, Mr. B and I grabbed a few group pictures with Southside. Luft, using his professional-looking SLR camera, took several personal shots for us in addition to the ones he shot during the interview.

Armed with the album cover from *Hearts of Stone*, I asked for an autograph, which he obliged. Retracing our route to exit the bus, we approached the front section and found Tony and Lisa sitting with the crew, casually drinking beer and watching a Clint Eastwood movie.

"You guys done already?" Tony said.

"What are you guys doing in here?" I said.

"They invited us to come in from the cold, so we did. We're watching a western."

"I could hear you guys talking inside," Lisa said. "That was sooo cool."

I was higher than a kite stepping out of the bus.

Making our way through the parking lot, Lisa grabbed my hand

and spun me around for a hug and a kiss. Maybe my master plan could still pay off in the end.

Returning to the car a little after 7:00, we celebrated with beers and a joint or two since the Jukes would be hitting the stage around 8:00. With our hands already stamped, we breezed past a few people waiting in line to pay the cover and grabbed spots at the bar. The place wasn't even half-filled.

"Kind of a small crowd, don't ya think?" I said to the bartender. "I thought there would be more people this close to showtime?"

"We're nowhere near showtime," he said. "Most people won't begin arriving until about 10:00."

10:00?

It was barely 7:30.

We got our drinks and headed to play some pinball. Since there was no formal coat check, people piled their jackets on the floor against the wall, so we followed suit.

Approaching the pinball machine, the distinct aroma of marijuana was wafting in the air. I looked toward the fumes and spotted a circle of people passing a joint around without a care in the world.

"You seeing this?" I posed to Mr. B.

Instead of responding verbally, he simply pointed to the front door. The bouncers were doing the same thing.

"Maybe we died and went to heaven?" he said, holding up the two joints in his hand.

This was shaping up to be a fascinating evening…

CHAPTER 5
THE DEBAUCHERY INSIDE THE FACTORY

Barbara and Kerri decided to make the trip after all, surprising us when they arrived close to 8:00, as did my friend John Colquhoun from New York Tech and his girlfriend, Janet. Colquhoun was an illustrator and columnist for *The Campus Slate*. He was also an official MIGS.

Although disappointed to learn about the later start time, they had a lot of catching up to do. Adding their coats to the rapidly growing pile on the floor, they headed for the bar. We still had two hours to kill before the show started, and with each passing minute, The Factory was getting more crowded.

With beers in the car, we spent considerable time shuttling back and forth between there and The Factory. The suddenly dropping temperatures outside starkly contrasted with the rising temperatures inside as The Factory approached maximum occupancy.

With show time approaching, we secured a spot near the stage, allowing us to be in a great position when the Jukes came on at 10:00. After a full day of drinking under my belt, preceded by the debauchery of the Stony Open, I mindlessly lost track of my brother. Mr. B was returning from the bathroom when he grabbed my arm and said he needed me to see something.

The scene in the game room area was out of control.

As we approached, people staggered around like zombies. The line to the women's room was twenty people deep. Groups surrounded both pinball machines while we spied a few stragglers slumped against the wall and passed out on the ever-growing pile of coats.

One of them was Tony.

"Let him sleep," I told Bruce. "He'll wake up when the Jukes hit the stage."

A little after 10:00, the house lights dimmed, and the stage lights came on, but the band emerging from the backstage area and strapping on their guitars wasn't the Jukes. Some other group was setting up. The Factory was hotter than hell and packed to the gills when the unannounced opening act began playing. That was our cue to grab our jackets and step outside (again) into the crisp night air.

"Oh, my God!" yelled Barbara, pointing to the growing crowd passed out on the mountain of coats, "Is that Tony? Is he okay?"

Despite assurances that he was fine, she insisted we prop him up and do some walking. So, we picked Tony up and guided him outside. Surprisingly, snow was beginning to fall—so much for the weatherman's prediction of a slight chance overnight.

After a few minutes, Tony perked up and told us he was napping.

The party in the back room was in full swing when we returned inside. Lisa got in line to the women's room, with about 25 people ahead of her.

"Do you want to go into the men's room?" I asked, "I'll stand watch."

She wanted no part of that. Considering the disgusting condition of the men's room, it was not a bad decision. It sported a 15-foot-long old-fashioned trough filled with ice for peeing. During the evening, a staff member periodically refills the quickly melting ice. Men were peeing everywhere, even occasionally hitting the trough.

The opening band finished close to 11:00, and the roadies took over to reset the equipment for the Jukes. We snaked through the masses near the bar for more drinks and smoked our last joint before the Jukes took the stage. The crowd was ready to blow the roof off.

Of course, the Jukes never disappoint. We joined the crowd in the middle of the dance floor, jumping up and down and generally enjoying ourselves. We would soon confirm that there were absolutely no rules at The Factory.

At some point, I headed back to the bathroom with Colquhoun. The line to the women's room was still a mile long. To our surprise, some chicks made their way inside the men's room. Instead of waiting for one of the three stalls, one was straddling the trough with her pants around her ankles.

I guess when you gotta go, you gotta go.

Meanwhile, The Factory was utterly out of control.

With the concert in full swing, I spied Luft standing with a group of strangers at one of the bistro tables near the pinball machines. He was grinning and holding up a gallon-sized plastic bag stuffed with reefer while some guy was rolling a joint that would have made Cheech and Chong proud.

Behind him were two girls surrounding the pinball machine, but they weren't playing. They were setting up lines of cocaine on the glass surface.

Strolling over to the entrance door, I poked my head outside and saw the snow accumulating. Someone would have to pilot The Beast home to Long Island, and I wasn't confident Mr. B would be up to the task. There was no way my brother could drive; that was for sure. And Luft? He was cooked.

Not that I was trying to be a hero or anything, but I slowed down a few hours ago. Part of my master plan included the ability to, well, let's say, perform. I was pacing myself, skipping a round now and then while sneaking in a glass of water for every two beers. Although joints were being passed around like M&M's, I was limiting my exposure.

CHAPTER 6
THE MASTER PLAN WORKED

As the Jukes broke into "Having a Party," I knew it was the final song before the encores and took that as my cue to start rounding up the group and vamoose out of Staten Island while we still could. It was after 1:00, and the last time I checked, the snow was falling harder.

I didn't get much resistance from our completely fried travelers. With limited options available for assigning a driver for The Beast, I volunteered myself and confiscated the keys from Tony, who happily relinquished them. Lisa sat in the front seat and tried to stay awake to keep me alert. Before we hit the bridge, Mr. B, Tony, and Luft were sawing wood. As we approached JFK Airport on the Belt Parkway, the snow changed from steady to heavy. By the time we reached Baldwin, the snow was accumulating at an alarming rate.

When we arrived at Lisa's apartment with the storm in full swing, Mr. B was the most coherent of the three. After a nap for over an hour, he took over the reins and drove Tony's car. I stayed with Lisa in Baldwin because she didn't want me to drive in the blizzard. Besides, Baldwin Sanitation had already plowed in my car, and I wasn't about to begin shoveling.

Finally, a plan that worked!

After dropping off Tony and The Beast (at my parent's house), Mr. B cleared the snow from his car, The Dent Mobile, and drove slowly back to his house on Pittsburgh Avenue. He had to work at 9:00 on Monday morning in the Safe Deposit area of the Dime Savings Bank in the Sunrise Mall.

The next day, the entire New York Metropolitan area woke up to 8-10 inches of snow.

Working in Safe Deposit was the perfect job for a hard-partying dude like Mr. B. There were plenty of small, closet-like privacy booths for customers. Mr. B had a sweet arrangement with his much older workmate, Tom McGann, a retired teacher. Sometimes, Mr. B would slip into a booth and lock the door for an hour or two of shuteye. He would return the favor, covering for McGann when he skirted the bank's rules by leaving the premises and grabbing a hot dog and a beer at Nathan's. One good turn deserves another.

After lunch, while Mr. B rested his eyes in a privacy booth, McGann woke him up because he had a phone call.

It was my father.

"Bruce, do you know where Paul is?" my father asked. "He didn't come home last night, and Anthony doesn't know where he is."

Of course, Tony had no idea where I was. He passed out in the back of his car the night before.

"Well, Mr. D," Bruce said, "I kind of know where he is. I think he's having some submarine races with his girlfriend."

"Oh, okay…"

CHAPTER 7
THE LAST BAD DECISION JEFF LUFT WOULD EVER MAKE

If this were a fairy tale, Jeff Luft would have been awarded MIGS status for life, and we would have forever been in his debt for getting us that interview. Who knows, we might have even become close friends.

But that's not what happened.

The Campus Slate is published every Tuesday, so having an article ready by the Monday deadline was out of the question, considering the debacle at The Factory the night before. Instead, we worked on it during the week and prepared it for the next issue. My editor liked it so much that he would feature the interview in the middle of next week's paper, spanning two pages with plenty of Luft's pictures.

However, after developing Luft's pictures, they were unusable.

All of them. Every fucking one of them.

Most were dark, out of focus, and off-center, making all the cool shots we posed for with Southside Johnny unrecognizable.

Of the over 30 pictures he took, only one was possibly salvageable, a closeup of Southside looking like he was underwater while answering a question and gesturing with his hand. My editor captioned the photo with my favorite response regarding a message for his fans about their new album, "If they don't buy the album, I'll kill them...."

Without pictures to accompany the article, it was reduced to a single page.

You would think that ruining a two-page spread because he failed to operate a camera properly would have been the worst thing Luft could have done to us. But you would have been wrong.

About two months later, Southside Johnny and the Jukes were

performing at the Calderone Concert Hall, a converted movie theatre in Hempstead, just a hop, skip, and a jump from our hometown. Having attended many other shows in this building, including the Jukes once or twice before, we pretty much knew our way around.

High off his triumphant score in getting us an interview with Southside, Jeff Luft wanted to redeem himself after the debacle with his picture-taking skills that almost led to his death.

One afternoon, he asked me, "How would you guys like to get backstage for the Southside concert at the Calderone?"

"Can you think of any reason I would turn that down?"

"I just spoke to his manager and got us two backstage passes."

"That's great, but since you said 'us,' I assume that includes you in the equation. Based on my limited math skills, that makes three of us."

"I know, but all I could get was two," he said. "You and I will go backstage, then I'll give you my pass, and you can go out and give it to Bruce."

"Why don't you just give me both of them and one of us will come out to get you?" I offered as an alternative.

"It doesn't work that way," he said. "The passes are in my name, so I have to go in with you after I pick them up."

Luft explained that the VIP passes must be picked up at the backstage entrance. From there, you go directly inside. The doorway was off the main parking lot in the back of the building. He had to present his ID to receive the passes.

I didn't like the sound of that one bit, but I had no choice. We chatted for a few more minutes to hammer out the logistics, arranging a meeting spot outside the back entrance to The Calderone around 7:00. That would give us plenty of time to hang out backstage with the other VIPs.

The Calderone was an old-fashioned converted movie theatre with a brightly lit marquee directly on Hempstead Turnpike, a busy road with limited parking. Most concertgoers used the generous free parking available in the back. The VIP entrance was down a small ramp utilized by trucks to bring in supplies and band equipment. It descended about 10 feet below street level. A single glass door, manned by a security guard, allowed access to the backstage area.

Mr. B and I arrived before 7:00 and hung out, waiting for Luft and the Golden Tickets. Other VIPs were happily picking up their passes and flashing the security guard, who just nodded and allowed them through. Having never been backstage for any reason, all we could talk about was who we might see there, what we might talk to people about, and, of course, how much free beer we would consume before being thrown out.

As 7:30 moved closer to 8:00, there was still no sign of Jeff Luft.

"Where the hell is this Hammerhead?" Mr. B said at one point.

"I have no fucking idea," I said, "But if he doesn't show up soon, he's a dead man."

By 8:00, we met up with our friends to pre-game at the cars and kept one or two eyes on the backstage door at all times, hoping to see Luft. No dice.

By the time we got into the building for the show, we were already three sheets to the wind. As the show progressed, all I could think about was the degree of physical pain I was going to bring to Luft the next time I saw him. I was so looking forward to getting backstage to meet Southside again. Anticipating a face-to-face meeting and hoping to secure an autograph, I even brought a printed copy of the article and folded it in my back pocket.

When the Jukes launched into their signature show-closing tune, "Having a Party," we made our way to the open area at the front of the stage to join all the other crazies dancing up and down like lunatics. The front of the concert hall was now wall-to-wall with nut jobs like us.

For a short time, I forgot all about Luft and enjoyed the music and the mayhem surrounding me.

That's when I spied Luft off-stage to the right, moving his head to the beat. He was cradling a beer bottle, surrounded by VIPs bopping around him.

I grabbed Mr. B by the head and swiveled his noggin toward Luft. "Do you see what I see?"

"Where?" he said.

"Behind the speakers," I told him. "Look over the shoulders of the bass player, where the muckety-mucks are standing–it's fucking LUFT!"

Mr. B was speechless for a few seconds. "That motherfucker! I'm going to kick his ass!!"

After the song ended, the band disappeared offstage as the crowd began chanting for an encore. Mr. B and I made our way to the right side of the stage, trying to get Luft's attention.

After screaming, "LUFT!!" at the top of our lungs a couple of times, he finally turned toward us, smiled, and waved as if nothing was wrong with this picture. He had one arm around a girl's waist and was waving to us like he was the Queen of England on a parade float.

I signaled for him to come over and talk to us, and he reluctantly began to make his way to the edge of the stage.

"I can't come out now," he said. "Meet me at the backdoor after the show." He returned to his primo spot as the band came out to do the encores.

During the encores, I could only think about that piece of shit enjoying free beer and access to the stage with all the other VIPs. On top of that, he gave the other ticket to some chick, most likely expecting to get laid.

Mr. B and I went to the backdoor area immediately after the show ended and descended the ramp, expecting Luft to meet us at the door, but he was nowhere to be found.

I tried to bargain with security, but I couldn't go in without a backstage pass; end of story. There was no room for negotiation.

"But the guy with my pass is already inside," I pleaded.

"That's too bad. I can't let you in without a pass," the guard said. "That's how it works."

"Can I at least look for him?" I asked.

"Sure," he said, "As long as you stand right there and don't open the door."

I put my forehead against the glass door and positioned my hand over my eyebrows to peer down the elongated hallway. Mr. B was shadowing me, mumbling things that would eventually get us in trouble. The security guard occasionally asked us to step aside so others with the proper passes could enter.

Mr. B had smoke coming out of his ears. "This is bullshit, man," he said to no one in particular.

Plenty of people walked past the hallway carrying drinks or plates of food, but none of them were Jeff Luft.

"Oh, my God!" I pointed to the glass, "It's Clarence Clemons!" Sure enough, Bruce Springsteen's saxophone player was part of the backstage party.

Just then, Luft drifted into view. He didn't have a care in the world and was standing around taking everything in with that same girl at his side.

"It's LUFT!!!!!"

Mr. B started banging on the door to get Luft's attention, but he ignored us.

"Stop that," the security guard said.

"That's him," Mr. B yelled, "That's the guy. LUFT!!!!"

"LUFT!" I yelled, "YOU FUCKING PIECE OF SHIT!!!"

With our voices echoing in the small tunnel, most of Long Island could have heard our cries. Luft didn't acknowledge us. Instead, he mysteriously slunk out of view.

That drove Mr. B off the rails.

"LUFT!" he kept screaming over and over.

Trying to reason with the guard was futile because he was no longer paying attention to me. He had his sights set on the raging Mr. B.

"I'm going to tell you one more time," he said to a now completely inconsolable Mr. B, "Stay away from the god-damned door."

Mr. B refocused on the guy's words and slowly walked away from the door.

As I turned to plead with the guy one more time, Mr. B came rushing to the door with smoke coming out of his ears. Instead of pounding on the door this time, he began kicking it out of frustration.

That led the security guard to grab and physically remove both of us, threatening to call the police if we didn't leave the area immediately.

Mr. B was livid, but that wouldn't get us anywhere now, so we returned to the parking lot for a beer and a joint to heal our wounds.

The new plan was to stake out the backstage entrance until Luft appeared. I wasn't sure what we would do, but I wanted to be present when it happened.

CHAPTER 8
THE AFTERMATH

About an hour after the show ended, several people walked up the ramp to their cars—still no Luft. I left Mr. B passed out in the passenger seat of my car and decided to go down the tunnel and get a Luft update.

Approaching the tunnel, I spied a different sentry manning the stool by the glass door. When a guy leaving the venue passed me on the ramp, I asked if the backstage party was over. He told me some people were still inside and offered me his backstage pass.

I happily took it and headed down to the door.

Flashing the pass as the professional yet inebriated journalist I was, he waved to me as I sped past him and into an almost empty room. Once, there was a bustling scene with musicians, friends, family, and one Jeff Luft, but only a few stragglers remained in conversation on a couch.

After walking around, I found a small refrigerator filled with Miller High Life (Southside's favorite, of course) and grabbed a cold one while I continued looking for Luft. Most of the food was long gone, but so was Luft. I snagged a handful of chocolate chip cookies and stuffed them in my pocket, sure I'd have the munchies on the way home.

I found Southside Johnny sitting by himself in one of the smaller rooms. He was nursing a beer and staring out into space. I waved to him from the door, and he waved back. Although it wasn't an invitation to join him, I did anyway.

I introduced myself as one of the people interviewing him at The Factory in Staten Island back in February, recalling some of the insane things we experienced as part of the audience that night. He just shook his head.

"Wow," he said, "That was a crazy night!"

I asked if he'd gotten a chance to read the article we wrote about him. He told me he reads many newspaper articles, so he probably did. I retrieved the folded page from my back pocket and presented it to him. He took one look at the picture with the caption, "If they don't buy the album, I'll kill them…" and laughed.

"Oh, yeah," he said, "I saw this one!"

Southside autographed it for me, and we chatted for a few more minutes. However, I sensed his exhaustion, so I politely thanked him. He then offered to meet with me again and suggested I call his manager to schedule another interview whenever we wanted.

I walked out on Cloud 9. There was only one thing left to do.

Find and destroy Jeff Luft…

CHAPTER 9
THE EXCOMMUNICATION OF JEFF LUFT

The next day, Mr. B and I worked on the Brewing Out column for the paper, detailing our concert experience at The Calderone and Jeff Luft's future death. Of course, we weren't really going to harm him, although Mr. B didn't think it was out of the realm of possibility.

"I have an idea," I said while trying to decide how to handle the Luft situation. "We can't really put into writing that we were plotting to kill him. What if we excommunicate him and revoke his MIGS status."

"It would be like a public execution," Mr. B said. "I like it but still want to wring his fucking neck."

"That day will come, my friend," I assured him. "He still needs to come into *The Slate* office to write his entertainment column, so I'll run into him sometime this week."

And so it goes. Luft was doomed.

On Tuesday, the New York Tech campus buzzed with news that Team FUBAR excommunicated Jeff Luft. Since the members of Team FUBAR were a mystery, I usually strolled around The Pub, where other students were reading and discussing the column. Nobody seemed to know Jeff Luft, but everyone was talking about him.

I stopped into *The Slate* office every day that week, but still no Jeff Luft. The editor said he hadn't heard from him and hadn't yet submitted his entertainment column. The following week, Luft was nowhere to be found again. I asked some other writers on the paper, but Luft was missing in action. Over the last few weeks left in the Spring semester, he never reappeared in *The Slate* office.

He was just gone…

This is the last known picture of Jeff Luft (upper row on the left, wearing a white turtleneck). In the middle are Mr. B and your humble narrator holding our "Team FUBAR" placards. I kept mine on the dashboard of my car and had Bruce Springsteen sign it when we met him. Of course, we're the only ones brandishing beers (Heineken).

PART FOUR

IT'S HARD TO BE A SAINT IN THE CITY

Studio 54 and the Wino

(April 1979)

PROLOGUE

Approaching our destination, the lizard cabbie pulled up to the curb under the Madison Square Garden marquee, directly in front of the stairs and escalators leading from the street level into the bowels of Penn Station. We only had a few minutes to make that final 2:30 am Babylon train, so time was of the essence. The next one didn't depart for another three hours.

Regrettably, my four compadres were still entangled in a friendly, full-scale wrestling match in the back of the oversized cab. As I opened the door, they spilled out onto the sidewalk, laughing and giggling like a bunch of schoolgirls before regaining their composure.

The Big Man got to his feet and grabbed Douglas under his left shoulder, lifting him off the pavement. "Come with me." He then turned to my brother Tony and Mr. B, who remained at ground level. "We'll run down and hold the doors until you guys get there." They descended the deserted steps two and three at a time, soon followed by the others, leaving me alone with the lizard cabbie.

My scrambled brain had no idea where the rotating numbers on the fare box finally stopped. Reaching into my pocket, hoping to locate President Andrew Jackson's smiling face and not George Washington's, I assumed ten bucks would cover the short trip, including a tip. I handed the crumpled paper to the lizard cabbie and hoped for the best.

CHAPTER 1
THE BEGINNING

How did we get into this situation?

It was a slow Saturday evening, to begin with. With nothing better to do, I was having a few adult beverages with my friends at our favorite watering hole, Jocelyn's. Bruce (Mr. B), Douglas Dower, the The Big Man always worked during the day on Saturday, but this was uncharted territory for my brother Tony and me. I usually worked all day Saturday (1:00 to 9:00) at Parts Place Plus in the Sunrise Mall, while my brother worked evenings in the restaurant at JC Penney. But they were doing some sort of inventory at JC Penney that day, and he worked early in the morning.

The Sunrise Mall had just begun opening on Sundays, and our store manager didn't want to work seven days a week. He assigned me to open the store every other Sunday, alternating with Patricia Riehl. That Friday, he had to attend a wedding and knew he would be in no shape to open on Saturday, so he asked if I could open the store and then have the night off. No problemo.

My brother and I joined our compadres after clocking out at 6:00, and we had a couple of pops before heading across the street to the Nautilus Diner to get something to eat. While waiting to pay the check at the register, Tony picked up a pocket-sized train schedule for the LIRR Babylon branch from the counter. He checked the weekend schedule inside the green-and-white pamphlet and noticed a train leaving the Massapequa Park station at 9:05 for Penn Station.

"You guys want to jump on the train and head into the city," he said to no one in particular. "There's a train leaving in about 45 minutes."

"We'll have to make a few quick stops and get some supplies," Douglas added.

"I think I have some hootch in my car," Mr. B said.

"I have rolling papers on me, but what about your cars?" I said, having traveled with Tony on our way to Jocelyn's.

"We'll go in The Beast and deal with that later," Tony said, volunteering to drive to the station.

My brother Tony drove my father's blue, 2-door 1965 Buick Skylark, nicknamed The Beast, after the Rolling Stones song, "Beast of Burden." The Beast served him (and us) well on previous adventures, but it was time to move on to bigger and better machines of destruction. Tony planned to pick up a white 1965 van the next day, making this our last journey in The Beast. The van would affectionately be called The White Whale.

Pressed for time, we headed to the local liquor store for Peppermint Schnapps and Southern Comfort and then to Foodtown for beer. Sadly, they didn't stock cold beer.

Staring at the cases sitting at room temperature on the shelves, Douglas reached into the paper bag camouflaging the already-opened bottle of Southern Comfort, took a swig, and announced, "This is bullshit. I'm not drinking warm beer."

"I got an idea," Mr. B said, procuring one of the empty cardboard boxes stashed nearby. "Look, instant coolers!"

With the clock ticking, we grabbed a case, some cardboard, and a couple of bags of ice. We were ready to go.

I rode shotgun while Mr. B and Douglas scrunched into the back seat along with The Big Man, two bags of rapidly melting ice, and cardboard boxes. Flying out of the Foodtown parking lot, we found the 9:05 already at the Massapequa Park station. Tony yelled, "Time for Plan B!" and instead gunned it down Sunrise Highway, racing the train to the next station.

Running parallel to the railroad tracks, Sunrise Highway offered us a straight run to surpass the approaching train and the ability to gauge how far ahead of it we were at any time. After all, we needed time to park, gather our essentials, and race to the elevated platform before the train pulled out.

The Massapequa LIRR station sat less than a half-mile west of Massapequa Park, too close to make up any significant ground. Hightailing it to the next station in Seaford, we were starting to gain an

IT'S HARD TO BE A SAINT IN THE CITY

advantage but still needed more distance. Tony piloted The Beast directly to Wantagh without slowing down or stopping.

On the way, Mr. B carefully planned our exit strategy like an Army General. We only had one shot at this. There wouldn't be time to regroup if we missed our opportunity at Wantagh. Sitting shotgun in the two-door Beast, I'd jump out of the car and bend down the front seat so Mr. B could bolt with the cardboard boxes and ice. Tony would do the same on the driver's side, allowing The Big Man to escape with the beer. Douglas would continue to drink heavily.

Racing into the parking lot, Tony swung The Beast into an empty spot not far from the staircase. Above our heads, the train was pulling into the station. It was now or never.

We executed General Patton's plan perfectly and began our race up the stairs. Halfway to the platform, a recorded announcement blared from inside the cars: "Please stand clear of the closing doors."

Gasping for breath and sweating like pigs despite the cool spring evening, we jumped into the closest car and grabbed a set of facing seats. Mr. B and The Big Man assembled the makeshift coolers, filled them with beer, and topped them off with ice. We toasted our timing and good fortune with our slightly chilled beers.

But the train doors still hadn't closed.

Poking my head out the still-open doors to investigate, two older women slowly ascended the stairs to the platform. When they reached the top, both sporting canes, they leisurely passed us and continued toward the middle of the train. The conductor held the train for them, rendering our rush up the stairs a waste of time and energy.

Even with all the remaining scheduled stops, we would arrive at Penn Station in less than an hour. Since we wanted to avoid dragging beer in wet cardboard boxes and melting ice through the streets of Manhattan, we needed to finish most, if not all, of what we had.

"So, what's the plan?" I asked while taking a slug of Peppermint Schnapps when the bottle made its way into my hand.

"There ain't no plan," Mr. B said as I handed him the schnapps.

"I'm open for anything," The Big Man said, grabbing a fresh one and twisting the cap off with minimal spillage.

Tony then piqued the interest of the entire group. "What about Studio 54?"

"You know we're not getting in, right?" I asked.

"I didn't say we were getting in. I just said we should go there. It's as good a destination as any."

Halloween 1979

So, we toasted to making our way to Studio 54 and continued our attack on the beer, which was growing colder by the minute, thanks to Mr. B's cardboard cooler idea.

Before we knew it, the outside light disappeared once inside the tunnel under the East River. In about ten minutes, we'd be pulling into Penn Station.

Approaching the station the train began to decelerate. Mr. B and The Big Man stashed the remaining few beer bottles in their jacket pockets. Looking back at our seats to ensure we had everything, I felt terrible for the next passengers. Cardboard boxes were never intended to hold melting ice and empty bottles.

Before heading to the surface, we stopped to take a quick supply inventory. Douglas reported half the schnapps gone, while Tony noted we had plenty of Southern Comfort. Mr. B had one beer in his pocket and one opened in his hand. Big Man and I finished off the last ones from his pockets.

We emerged at the Eighth Avenue end of Madison Square Garden, stopping at the deli across the way for a few cold six-packs. Assuming Studio 54 was somewhere on 54th Street, we headed uptown for the 20-block trek.

CHAPTER 2
THE SHENANIGANS OUTSIDE OF STUDIO 54

A giant black marquee towered over the entrance, displaying the iconic "54" in bright white. A long line of people dressed to the nines stretched far beyond the entranceway, encroaching on the municipal parking garage next door.

Eyeballing the different types of people waiting to gain access, it was apparent that five drunk guys wearing T-shirts, jeans, and sneakers weren't getting in.

I had to pee like a racehorse. A public bathroom stood inside the garage, and I instructed the troops to follow me for a pit stop while we plotted our next move. It was well-lit and not the grungy degenerate hangout I was expecting.

Time became irrelevant at this stage in the evening, not that we cared. Planting ourselves on the sidewalk outside the garage entrance, we settled in to finish off our current stash of alcohol before Big Man headed out for a beer run with Douglas to the nearest deli.

Our location provided a perfect position to comment on every rejected loser and make them suffer additional humiliation as they passed us. With our personal bathroom only a few steps away, we could people-watch and drink as long as we wanted.

While doing his business, Mr. B encountered an African-American wino even more wasted than us. He was thin, almost emaciated, with a salt and pepper beard that hadn't been trimmed in decades, appearing much older than his years. Like Indiana Jones once said, "It ain't the years; it's the mileage." Mr. B invited him to join our little soirée. Although we never found out his name, we tried to convince him that we were the Ramones who happened to be performing that night downtown at the Palladium.

"I hearda you guys!" he warbled, taking a swig from his disgusting wine bottle. "If you guys are really dem, sing me a damn song!"

We broke into an acapella version of "Rockaway Beach," which wasn't too convincing.

"I'm not sure who dem Romans are, but damn, you guys are good!"

Douglas offered him some of our remaining Southern Comfort, deftly pouring it into his wine bottle. At least for this evening, he had some friends to hang out with.

Once our wino friend left, things started spiraling out of control.

Several limousines shuttling what we assumed were big shots began to show up. Sometimes, the people emerging would get inside Studio 54; sometimes, they didn't. A limo stopped across from us, and three beautiful women emerged, struggling to walk in high heels and platform shoes. A few minutes later, they dejectedly returned. One of them wore a sports coat, and as she passed, turning in our direction, she opened her jacket to reveal no shirt underneath. Flashing her tits, she said, "Can you believe they wouldn't let me in?"

How do you reject a topless chick with a kick-ass rack?

IT'S HARD TO BE A SAINT IN THE CITY

Later, another limo pulled up to the curb. Two important-looking people sporting suits and ties exited the vehicle along with the driver, making their way to the entrance and leaving the still-idling vehicle unattended.

"You think those guys are getting in?" I asked my brother as he slugged the last of the Southern Comfort.

Tony turned to me with a devilish grin on his face.

Like John Belushi's Bluto in Animal House, I almost expected him to raise one eyebrow. Although not nearly as rotund, Tony did resemble Belushi. Our friend Joe Piti, who bore a striking resemblance to the much taller Dan Aykroyd, paired with Tony to impersonate "The Blues Brothers" one Halloween, coming in First Place at a Baldwin bar called Salem's Lot and winning a massive basket of cheer.

Joe Piti and my brother Tony

"Who cares if they get in? They left the car running. I'm going to take it for a spin around the block."

"I'm going with you," Douglas said as he tried to rise from a sitting position on the curb, only to have gravity decide for him.

Tony made his way to the driver's side of the idling limo and was surprised to find the door unlocked. At the same time, the driver returned bug-eyed and shouting obscenities. He grabbed Tony by the shoulders and yanked him away from the door, but not before he pinched a sharpie from the dashboard as a souvenir.

Soon, the two former occupants headed dejectedly back to the limo, losers, just like everyone else.

"Aw, fellas," said The Big Man sarcastically, "couldn't get in?"

"Fuck you, assholes," one of them yelled back while returning to the sanctity of the inside and slamming the door.

CHAPTER 3
THE PENCIL-THIN JOINT

I needed to pee again, so I returned to our private john. Pulling the door open, I found two guys smoking one of the thinnest joints I had ever seen. Somehow they snuck by us and into the bathroom while we were conversing with our new wino friend. One thing is for sure: they were totally wasted.

They resembled Laurel and Hardy, as one was taller and thinner than the short, stocky guy. Both wore collared button-down shirts with the first couple of buttons undone. The taller "Stan" wore a bright white shirt with a medallion dangling from a gold chain, taking up the space on his exposed chest. The rounder "Ollie" donned a dark blue silk shirt with no hanging jewelry but sported a patch of thick, black hair.

While I proceeded to the urinal to do my business, they started conversing with me when Tony showed up. Soon, the four of us were chatting like old friends. Somehow, these two dudes got inside Studio 54, telling us about the $12 cover charge. Can you imagine paying $12 just to walk into a bar?

Stan whipped out another of those tiny joints to share during our talk, and we joined them, figuring we couldn't fathom being more fucked up than we already were. After a few hits apiece, The Big Man came crashing in to do his business and helped us finish it off.

Thanking Stan and Ollie for their hospitality, we headed back outside. To our surprise, Douglas and Mr. B were nowhere to be found. The two paper bags containing the empty beer cans were there, but they were not.

Tony pointed to a red neon sign across the street in a storefront window that said, "Bar."

Of course. Where else would they be?

Opening the door, we discovered them leaning against the bar with fresh bottles of Budweiser in their hands.

This was a classic "dive" bar, sitting directly across from one of the world's most famous nightclubs, packed with people like us who would never be allowed into a place like Studio 54. In the far corner, a comedian told jokes on a small stage. The crowd mostly ignored him, but we couldn't resist breaking his balls.

The Big Man and Mr. B were laughing way too loudly at his unfunny punchlines, getting more laughs than the comedian. He then launched into a joke about a fire in an apartment building in Pittsburgh. Douglas recognized it immediately and whispered something to Mr. B.

"A young boy was being dangled by his mother from a window in the burning building when he slipped from her grip," the guy said. "Just then, Lynn Swan, the Hall of Fame receiver for the Pittsburgh Steelers, happened to be walking by. Swan reaches out and catches the boy before he hits the ground and saves his life!"

The comedian then paused for dramatic effect.

"Then he spikes him," Mr. B yelled before the poor schmuck could deliver the punchline.

"Oh, you've heard that one," he said as the rowdy crowd began booing him off the stage. Mr. B and Douglas had huge smiles on their faces.

Making my way around to the other side of the bar, I found a pinball machine in one of the back corners. As a Silverball aficionado, I like to read the game instructions when playing an unfamiliar machine. They contain helpful tips for getting extra points or securing multi-ball action. When I stepped up to read them, something strange happened.

I couldn't make out the words.

Although I had plenty to drink, the letters on the paper buried under the glass were floating and beginning to resemble Egyptian Hieroglyphics. I leaned closer to them and squinted as if that would help. It didn't.

Popping in a quarter, I absent-mindedly shot the ball around the top. While it bounced around, I located the flipper buttons on the sides and banged them a few times to get the feel of the action. Watching intently as the ball ricocheted among the upper bumpers, I focused on the flashing lights and ringing bells more like a spectator than a player. As gravity took over, guiding the ball down the board, I watched helplessly as it bounced from one dead, lifeless flipper to the other, rolling into the chasm below.

Then I reacted and hit the flipper.

It seemed my motor skills were severely compromised. Maybe there was a reason those guys in the bathroom were so wasted. What was in that tiny joint?

The Big Man sauntered to join me at the machine and experienced the same sense of helplessness as ball after ball missed the flippers. Out of frustration, I must have banged on the glass a little too hard, drawing the attention of anyone within a hundred feet. The bartender yelled that he would throw us out if we didn't calm down. At this point, calming down was probably not part of the plan. I waved back to him, indicating everything was cool, and made an executive decision for our group—finish our beers, hit the can, and exit stage right.

The Big Man and I stumbled back to the bar to find our cohorts, and in time, we saw them exiting the bathroom with huge smiles. Citing "youthful exuberance," they told us they punched a few holes in the wall as a going-away present. Not to be outdone, The Big Man and I entered the head with the Devil's hands. It's hard to be a Saint in the city, you know.

By now, colors and bright lights were filling my head, and I vaguely remember him tearing off the toilet seat and stuffing it inside his jacket for a souvenir. Since it was now close to 2:00 am, we had to get out of Dodge quickly to make the last train back to Wantagh.

Hailing a large-capacity cab, everyone piled into the back. Mr. B, Douglas, and The Big Man spread out over the back while Tony and I sat on the tiny side seats facing backward. Big Man reached under his coat and produced his prized toilet seat, handing it to me for safekeeping. I promptly placed it around my neck.

Still buzzing from the aftereffects of the pencil-thin joint, I leaned over into the front and chatted with the driver about Hunter S. Thompson's book *Fear and Loathing in Las Vegas*. Suddenly, I was channeling the gonzo journalist. I looked at the cabbie's face as he spoke; his features were morphing from human to lizard.

Without warning, the other four maniacs in the back started pushing each other. Soon, we had a full-scale brouhaha in the cab's backseat as it headed down Seventh Avenue. The lizard-like cabbie never broke stride. Something told me he weathered this type of storm previously. A little rumble in the back is not much to sneeze at when you drive for a living in Jungleland.

CHAPTER 4
THE DISTURBANCE AT PENN STATION

Fighting through the mayhem in the back seat once we arrived at Penn Station, I stepped over bodies, opening the door to escape as the wrestling maniacs spilled out onto the concrete behind me. The Big Man grabbed Douglas off the sidewalk, and they ran down the stairs to hold the train for the rest of us. While rummaging through my pockets, searching for money to pay the lizard cabbie, Tony and Mr. B got to their feet, composed themselves, and raced to catch up with the others.

Approaching the entrance, Mr. B tossed Tony a beer bottle he found in his jacket pocket, catching the attention of a police officer. Initially ignoring the four inebriated individuals rolling out of the back seat of a yellow cab, the cop yelled for them to stop. Instead, they sped down the stairs. I froze as the scene unfolded.

Once Tony reached the bottom, The Big Man and his 6-1 250-pound frame appeared out of nowhere and blindsided him. Tony flipped ass over tea kettle, crashing to the tile floor while the bottle of beer shattered in his hand. With an officer descending after them, they scrambled in different directions to avoid being caught.

They disappeared from my sight as I chose the escalator for my long, slow descent. Having witnessed the police chasing my friends, I tried my best not to be noticed. Someone would need a straightforward yet foggy head to bail them out of jail. The cops were right behind them, communicating between the static on their walkie-talkies.

As I descended, two cops were staring at me. They couldn't possibly know I was with those lunatics causing such a ruckus, so I calmly walked past them, nodding my head, and offered a quick,

"Officers, how are you this fine evening?" As I strode by triumphantly, one of them called out, "Hey, you!"

Gradually, I turned to face them and said, "Yes?"

"Where are you going?"

"Home, officer. Why do you ask?"

"Well, just wondering why you have a toilet seat around your neck?"

Busted.

They had me cold, walking through Penn Station drunk and with a disgusting toilet seat around my neck.

"Oh, this old thing?" I said with a smile, removing the toilet seat and delicately placing it on the floor.

Without saying another word, I turned and kept walking. He was more concerned about the four maniacs running amok than some idiot with a toilet seat around his neck.

Someone whispered my name as I stood before the small TV displaying the departing train lines by color and track number. I spied The Big Man and Douglas peeking through the LIRR bathroom corridor opening and gave them a thumbs up. I continued my walk of innocence and made my way to Track 17. Sure enough, Tony hid behind a pole while Mr. B pretended to talk on a payphone as a cop walked past him. They pulled it off!

Once safely aboard the eastbound Babylon train, we settled into a set of facing seats, still wired from escaping the grasp of New York's Finest. The Big Man was eyeing one of the poster-sized advertisements on the interior retaining wall near the doors. The ad was for a law firm and contained images of the partner's smiling faces.

"Those guys are staring at us."

He ambled over to it and decided to remove the cardboard ad from the wall, slightly tearing it and bringing it back to our seats.

"Anybody got a pen?"

Tony reached into his jacket and produced the sharpie stolen from the idling limo outside Studio 54, which The Big Man happily took possession of. Soon, he was drawing pornographic images across the smiling faces while we laughed long and loud, making a general nuisance of ourselves in the mostly empty car.

Tony turned the cardboard advertisement over to the blank side and drew a rudimentary Hangman platform and a series of lines underneath to guess the letters. Now, we were deeply involved in a game of perverted hangman.

As we guessed the letters and shouted obscenities, the conductor made his way to our group and threatened to have us arrested at the Jamaica station, where the police would be waiting for us.

Bummer.

By the time we got to Jamaica, we had calmed down considerably to the point that The Big Man passed out. Employing that devious, mischievous, Belushi-like smile, Tony removed the cap from the stolen sharpie and stealthily approached the now-snoring giant beside him. He gently wrote, in big letters, "I M GAY" on the fingers of his left hand and "HOMO" on the right.

Each letter Tony administered brought more and more anticipation of him waking up and killing us. It was not unlike what the Lilliputians might have experienced when approaching and subduing a sleeping Gulliver. Eventually, he might find out what happened, but the Lilliputians scored a massive victory for now!

CHAPTER 5
THE LAST RUMBLE IN THE BEAST

Sometime around 3:30 am, our train pulled into Wantagh, and we decided to hit the Jack in the Box in Copiague for a late snack. Other than White Castle, which features gastronomic belly bombers, Jack in the Box was the only other fast-food place open 24 hours a day. Besides, they had a clown you could talk to manning their drive-thru.

Piling into the back of the Beast, we proceeded to Lindenhurst for tacos and burgers. This time, Mr. B rode shotgun, and I was part of the back-seat trio, flanked by Douglas and The Big Man.

Douglas couldn't contain himself any longer. He was chuckling as he pointed to The Big Man's hands. "Hey, what's that on your fingers?"

Not a good idea.

Being situated closest to Gulliver, I took the brunt of his vengeance before it turned into another full-scale rumble. Mr. B jumped over from shotgun to join the fracas. Unlike the New York City cabbie, Tony couldn't operate with all that commotion in his vehicle, so he pulled the Beast onto the shoulder of Sunrise Highway and joined the fray.

While we were rumbling and destroying the interior of the Beast, which was history after tonight anyway, Douglas decided to add some spice to the equation. He stuck his leg into the car's front seat, aiming for the gear shift on the steering wheel's neck, and kicked the lever of the still-idling vehicle into "Drive" with his foot.

With the driver's door still open, the Beast slowly began rolling down the shoulder with everyone wrestling in the backseat. Realizing we were suddenly in motion, Tony snapped into action. From the passenger side in the back seat, he released the latch on the front seat and folded it down. Rolling over it, he opened the passenger door of the slow-moving vehicle and circled around the back, running stride for stride with the Beast. Reaching for the open door, he jumped back into the driver's seat, seamlessly resuming the trek to Jack in the Box while the Donnybrook continued behind him.

For this early morning stop, we opted to skip the drive-thru and eat inside the restaurant instead of the car. I pity anyone who set eyes on us in Jack in the Box that night. We left with five maniacs and returned with five maniacs, which was all that mattered. However, I felt sorry for the poor slob expecting to use the toilet seat in that bar across from Studio 54.

While we sat at the table in a semi-conscious state, The Big Man glanced at the clock on the wall and reached for a napkin to wipe some errant ketchup from his lips, mumbling, "This is not good. Right about now, my alarm is going off. My father is going to wake up in about five minutes and yell for me to shut off the alarm. Then he's going to walk across the hallway to my room, open the door, and find out I'm not there."

I noticed the sun coming up and pointed it out to the group.

The Big Man snatched a french fry and blindly dipped it into a blob of ketchup sitting on the paper wrapper the burger came in, slowly rolling it in the condiment. Before taking a bite, he pointed it toward the window and the rising sun.

"Uh, oh. Here comes tomorrow…"

PART FIVE

FIVE MILES TO THE TURNPIKE

The Tale of the White Whale

(May 1979)

CHAPTER 1
THE WHITE WHALE

Not the ACTUAL White Whale but a reasonable facsimile.

In the spring of 1979, my brother Tony purchased a white 1964 Chevy G10 "Handy" Van, paying $250 in cash to the boyfriend of a coworker from JC Penney. The van came equipped with a manual transmission and a gear shift on the steering column. Unfortunately, he had never driven a manual transmission, regardless of the location of the gear shift. When he picked it up, my friend Bruce (Mr. B) accompanied him, giving him a crash course in how (and when) to change gears. As a neophyte, Tony was prone to grinding many of the jalopy's remaining gears to their limits.

Assigning your car a nickname was all the rage back then. Tony's first car, which came from my father, was crowned "The Beast of Burden." One look at this monstrosity's size, shape, and color was a no-brainer: it would forever be known as "The White Whale."

The Whale sported a "mid-engine," located in the middle of the vehicle instead of the front or rear. Access to the engine was through a raised compartment nestled between the driver and passenger seats. The windshield was directly above the bumper. It had the look and feel of a city bus. Tony would say looking out the giant window was like watching a movie.

It had previously been in an accident at some point, causing the front panel to be damaged. The repair shop deployed a technique where they drilled holes into the metal and used a bar to pull on it and pop out the dents. The procedure works very well, but the drilled holes are usually filled with putty and then sanded and painted once completed. That wasn't the case with the Whale. These holes were filled with an orange-tinted putty but never painted, leaving a pattern resembling machine gun fire. Tony liked it so much that he never fixed it.

Two windowed "suicide" doors, located on the passenger side, opened outward for entering and exiting the van compartment. It's not recommended that riders open them while the vehicle is in motion, as they will fly open, taking you with them, ergo the moniker of suicide doors.

The exterior on the driver's side had no additional windows or doors but sported a giant dent, resulting from being T-Boned by a motorcycle. The indentation clearly showed the motorcycle's front tire, the width of the handlebars, and what appeared to be the rider's head. It was hard to tell from the imprint whether he wore a helmet, but from all indications, he hit the van mid-air.

The only permanent seats in the Whale were for the driver and the passenger, separated by the mid-engine hump access cover. However, it came equipped with a mattress on top of a wooden platform in the rear, built about ten inches off the floor for storage. You can store stuff underneath the platform when opening the two windowed doors in the back.

Tony eventually customized the interior, replacing the disgusting, worn-out mattress with fresh foam rubber and covering it with bed sheets. Our mother chipped in with custom curtains for the side and back windows. He christened the back of the driver's seat to include a bumper sticker that said, "And on the Eighth Day, God created Bruce Springsteen."

Tony installed a radio/cassette player combo in a cubby hole above the driver's side of the dashboard. For sound, he put two speakers in the front panels and added large box speakers to the back of the Whale, storing them under the platform and adorning them with long wire extensions. This allowed for relocation outside when parked. It was the sweetest setup ever.

While the Whale's exterior may have resembled a weathered

Mexican transport vehicle capable of smuggling 30 people into the USA, the inside was customized for debauchery.

During the few years Tony owned the Whale, there were plenty of adventures. But this story chronicles the maiden voyage.

Tony and Mr. B in the ACTUAL White Whale.

CHAPTER 2
THE KEG

Six Flags Great Adventure theme park in New Jersey (exit 7A off the NJ Turnpike) was promoting its second annual "Senior Night" for New Jersey high school seniors. Southside Johnny and the Asbury Jukes would perform two shows that night, included with the price of admission. Tony volunteered his new wheels for this road trip.

We witnessed the Jukes for the first time in a live performance at Great Adventure the year before, during the first "Senior Night" promotion. Packing six of us in my Chevy Nova, we arrived late in the afternoon loaded for bear, stocked with sandwiches, beer, and, of course, many joints.

With time to kill before the 7:00 show, so we did some recon in the park to better understand the layout. However, the park was so crowded that we retreated to the car to party, returning before the show. Besides, we had grossly miscalculated how much beer we would need and ran out early.

We were already wasted when the Jukes took the stage inside the Great Arena for the first show. To be honest, the Great Arena wasn't that great. It was a small horseshoe-shaped venue with a stage at the open end. Concrete bleachers surrounded the dance floor. The Jukes played a 60-minute set like nothing we had ever seen. The energy and the music hooked us on the first song, "This Time It's For Real." We jumped and danced the entire time.

The Jukes came as advertised—a great bar band.

By the time the second show started at 11:00, we were cooked. We spent two hours stumbling around in a fog and ogling the High School senior chicks—at least, we hoped they were high school seniors. We found plenty of kiosks that sold beer to keep us hydrated.

When the Jukes retook the stage, the crowd thinned to about half its original size. Not that it mattered to us. Nobody remembered the trip home, but somehow, we ended up in Manhattan and couldn't figure out how to navigate off the island.

Learning our lesson from 1978, when we returned the following year with the Whale, we had a foolproof plan to prevent us from running out of beer.

Tony, Mr. B, and I went to Adolf's the night before to pick up the beer. There would be eight of us on this trip, including the girls, so calculating the number of beers needed for an entire day of debauchery was difficult.

Bruce's brother Peter the Mooch, The Big Man, and my friend from college, John Colquhoun, were on board, along with Barbara Dower and her friend Kerri Barr. Barbara and Kerri would be driving separately in Barbara's MG, taking no chances of being delayed by our shenanigans. The plan was to load the Whale with "supplies" and meet them at the Dower's house at 8:30 am to caravan to New Jersey.

"Why don't we just get a keg?" Tony said. "We can set it up in the van and not worry about coolers and running out of beer."

Not sure of New York State traffic law, but I had to ask the obvious question. "Can we put a tapped keg in a van while driving?"

"As long as we don't get caught," Mr. B said, "I don't see why not."

Doing the math, a half-keg held about 180 12-oz cups, give or take the expected spillage. The setup had a round, oversized plastic green tub, and a metal tapping apparatus. Weighing over 150 pounds, it took two of us to lift the keg. (Where is The Big Man when you need him?)

Since the keg was already cold, we set it up in my backyard and tapped it. We had to make sure it worked, right? Although we had quite a few beers, we barely made a dent in it. To keep it cool, we covered it with a blanket overnight.

The next morning, Tony emptied the melted ice water from the tub, and we moved the contraption into the van. Positioning it directly behind the driver's seat, the mid-engine hub partially obscured the tub from the outside world.

Wedged in this position would also secure it from rolling around as it became lighter. Jumping in my car, I ventured out for two blocks of ice and more bags of cubes, securing them in a cooler to prevent premature melting. I chipped away at the block with a hammer and screwdriver, and after a few minutes, we were ready to go!

Sitting shotgun, I poured fresh beers for Tony and myself, and we clinked the plastic cups, toasting our upcoming adventure.

Colquhoun arrived on time at my parent's house. As he walked toward the front door, Tony beeped the squeaky horn to let him know we were already in the van on the driveway.

Opening the side door so he could enter, he spied the keg as I poured him a beer. "What the fuck?"

"It's the only way to travel," I told him.

We picked up Mr. B and the Mooch, who quickly joined us for early morning beers, then went to collect The Big Man.

The Big Man was smiling like a kid on Christmas. "Are you fucking kidding me!"

"It's the only way to travel," I repeated, handing him a fresh one.

The next stop was to meet Barbara and Kerri at the Dower's house. Upon arriving, we noticed Doug's GTO in the driveway. He should have been at work already.

"I thought Doug had to work?" Mr. B asked.

"He's not gonna make it today," Barbara said. "He was drinking all night and is still passed out."

With a gleam in his eyes, Mr. B said, "I bet he doesn't know we have a keg."

"Probably won't matter. He's dead to the world."

Mr. B wasn't about to take no for an answer. He ran upstairs to rouse Douglas but to no avail.

"I tried, but he said no chance," Mr. B informed us upon returning to the Whale. "I even told him we have a keg. He's burnt toast."

"I got an idea," Tony said, handing Mr. B an empty red plastic cup. "Seeing is believing!"

Mr. B tapped a beer, and we all headed up to Douglas's bedroom as a team to help persuade him. After gently shaking him a few times, he still refused to open his eyes. Mr. B maneuvered the cup under his nose, lightly brushing the foam against his lips.

"Douglas," he said with a sly smile, "There's a fresh keg of this in Tony's van. How can you pass this up?"

Doug opened one eye and took a sip. It was like cracking amyl nitrate. Snapping awake, he downed the beer and said, "I'll be down in a minute."

CHAPTER 3
THE EAGLE HAS LANDED

Nothing will ruin your day like New York traffic.

There aren't too many ways off Long Island and into New Jersey by car, to begin with, so the choices are simple. Heading north through the Bronx gets you to the George Washington Bridge and over the Hudson River. For the adventurous, cutting through midtown Manhattan and using the Lincoln Tunnel allows you to go under the Hudson, although neither route is considered viable during daylight hours. The direct way was staying on the South Shore and traveling through Brooklyn and Staten Island.

Unfortunately, once you have committed to the southern route, there is no turning back. The 17-mile trek on the Belt Parkway from Kennedy Airport through Brooklyn and across the Verrazano Bridge into Staten Island is one of the most frustrating routes known to modern man. Moses and the Israelites had an easier time crossing the desert and might have made better time.

With me as the shotgun-riding copilot, the others began to settle into the belly of the White Whale. Mr. B positioned himself on the hub covering the mid-engine, assuming the role of keg master while doling out beers as needed. Peter and Douglas nestled on the edge of the bed as Colquhoun sat cross-legged, leaning against the driver's side wall. The Big Man took the spot atop the cooler, holding the additional ice. Everyone was enjoying the fresh, cold, tapped beer.

We were making excellent time until we approached Kennedy Airport.

"Oh, shit," Tony said as we crossed under the LIRR train trestle to make the sharp right turn heading west. A sea of red taillights arranged neatly in three distinctive rows glowed in front of us.

"Any ideas?" I said to no one in particular.

Mr. B grabbed my half-empty cup and topped it off before

morphing into John Belushi's "Bluto" character from *Animal House*. "I suggest you begin drinking heavily."

Who was I not to take his advice?

One of the best things about having a keg in the van was not worrying about what to do with the empties. We filled our cups and chugged away. Of course, the primary problem down the road might be spillage, but for now, it wasn't much of a concern. That said, ice sitting in a tub turns to water quickly inside a vehicle without air conditioning, even in the middle of May.

Did I mention the Whale didn't have air conditioning?

The Whale possessed overhead vents, and we had the front windows open, but unless you are traveling at highway speed, there isn't any airflow while sitting in traffic.

Conveniently stuck in the lane next to us, Barbara and Kerri weren't going anywhere in their MG either. Douglas opened one of the suicide doors and passed two fresh beers to them. We made an executive decision to keep that door open, allowing for better airflow.

Along the way, other people stuck along with us wanted in on the festivities and were also signaling for beers, so Douglas occasionally obliged. It was the neighborly thing to do.

It took over two hours to get to the bridge, across the Arthur Kill Straight via the Goethals Bridge, and into the fresh air of the refineries in New Jersey. We were partially loaded as we approached the New Jersey Turnpike (I-95), and things were beginning to spiral out of control. Tony pulled into the Grover Cleveland rest stop for cheaper Jersey gas while giving us the most opportune chance to pee.

Now mired in the day's heat, we decided to keep one side door open once we hit the turnpike. No longer burdened by New York traffic, the air (and the beers) flowed nicely through the Whale. With Tony's custom sound system, we had our choice of cassette tapes, but we voted to stay with the radio, specifically WNEW-FM (102.7). We had about 60 miles until we arrived at Exit 7A for Great Adventure, finding a few flaws in the "keg-in-a-van" theory along the way.

Not to get too scientific, but the water level in the tub rose every time we added more ice. For starters, when the Whale changed lanes or hit a dip in the road, it crested the sides and spilled onto the floor.

FIVE MILES TO THE TURNPIKE

There was also an optics problem while driving at highway speed down the Jersey Turnpike with the doors open for ventilation. We'd wave to people passing us on the passenger side as they stared in disbelief when realizing a full-sized keg was part of our cargo.

When reaching exit 7A, we drove around the cloverleaf leading to Route I-195, about ten miles from Great Adventure. After ponying up the Turnpike toll, Tony maneuvered the Whale to a grassy knoll so the passenger side was not visible from the plaza.

We spilled out (literally) and had a group urination experience.

After returning the rented beer to nature, we returned to the Whale as the Joe Jackson song "Is She Really Going Out With Him?" came on the radio. It reminded John Colquhoun of his messy breakup with his girlfriend, who chose someone else over him. To help ease the pain, Douglas tapped a fresh beer for him while we all screamed the lyrics along with poor John.

As we piled back into the belly of the Whale to continue our journey, Tony suggested we dump all the water out of the tub to prevent additional spillage.

"Nonsense," Douglas said. "We need to keep some ice water in the tub because the cold water keeps the fresh ice from melting too quickly."

Suddenly, I felt like I was on *Gilligan's Island*, and Douglas was The Professor.

Douglas grabbed another bag of cubes from the cooler and poured those suckers around the base of the keg. There were still two more bags of cubes and another block left. That's when I noticed The Big Man's rear end was soaked.

"What happened," I asked. "Did you piss yourself?"

"Not yet," Mr. B chimed in.

Peter, studying to be a chemical engineer at Clarkson University, asked, "How did you piss yourself from behind?"

It turns out The Big Man, although he had a wet ass, might have been the smartest. While the rest of us were sweating, he used the cooler as his seat. Nothing like a wet, cold ass on a hot summer day.

Colquhoun had the best idea. He scooped a cup out of the tub, bent his head out the side door, and doused himself. We took that as a cue and, before long, followed his lead and dumped ice water over our own heads. This served to cool us off and helped lower the water level in the tub.

Somewhere along I-95, we got separated from Kerri and Barbara, imagining Kerri yelling, "Where the hell are those assholes?" We knew we weren't too far behind and would locate them in the parking lot. If not, there was a pretty good chance they would find us. After all, the Whale would stick out like a giant, white sore thumb in a field populated with residential cars.

Arriving sometime after 2:00 pm, we weren't in a rush to go inside the park when we had a van containing a keg at our disposal. The lot was about half filled, so we circled until we found a light pole we could park near to use as a landmark later. The poles contained signs with numbers to help locate your car when returning.

Six Flags provided free transportation via tram to and from the distant front gate. Surveying the situation and looking at our surroundings through a drunk, naked eye, it seemed like a good idea to remember where you parked your car, or in this case, a giant white van. For future reference, I mentally noted 23 on the light pole near the Whale.

I even mentioned it to Mr. B as a backup. "We're near light pole 23. Try and remember that."

"How am I supposed to remember that?"

He had a point. I decided to tell everyone in our party, hoping someone would recall "23" later in the evening. Barbara took a piece of paper from her tiny pocketbook and wrote it down. You can always count on women when the chips are down.

The trip took more than four hours, but in Neil Armstrong's immortal words, "The Eagle has Landed."

Mr. B rolled a couple of joints, and we quaffed a few more beers. We covered the keg in a blanket to avoid being busted should a bystander peer into the window and feel compelled to notify the local authorities. Despite the day's heat, the ice blocks held much better shape than the cubes. Although the initial cubes melted, the new bag performed quite nicely in cold water.

It turns out The Professor was right again.

CHAPTER 4
GREAT ADVENTURE AND THE JUKES

Grabbing a fresh round of beers, we waited under the shaded overhang where the tram stopped to pick up and discharge passengers. We were the only ones there. The main entrance to the park was so far away it wasn't visible from our location.

"We going on any of the rides?" I asked innocently.

"Not me," said Douglas.

Colquhoun raised his index finger as if asking permission to talk in a classroom. "I'd like to do Lightning Loops."

Tony wiped the sweat from his forehead onto the sleeve of his already-drenched shirt and took a swig of the cool Nectar of the Gods. "I hope they have a water ride."

"I thought there was a water ride near the place where the Jukes played when we came last year," I offered. "Then again, that was a very foggy evening…"

Mr. B removed the two rolled joints from his pants and placed them in the folds of his wallet. "I better put them in here so I don't crush them in my pocket. If we do find a water ride, they'll stay dry."

Looking around at our current isolated situation, I had a better idea. "Maybe we should just smoke one before we go in?"

"I second that emotion," The Big Man said.

The courtesy tram arrived just as we put the finishing touches on the joint and provided transport directly to the Grand Plaza. Instead of heading to the ticket booth, we went into the grassy area and finished the other joint. Of course, that made purchasing the admission tickets a little foggy, but we each paid $9.95 (including tax) and went in with smiles on our faces and a nickel in our pockets.

Guided by the knowledge of the park layout we gained from our previous excursion to Great Adventure, it helped us navigate quickly to the Great Arena at the far end of the park, to the left of the main gate. Concession stands, bathrooms, and the water-based Log Flume ride were nearby.

A massive chain-linked set of double doors, stretching ten feet high, guarded the entrance at the closed end of the horseshoe with a six-foot green privacy screen embedded in the fence links. Nobody could see over it except The Big Man, who stood on his tiptoes.

After trekking across the park in the heat of the day, some of us decided to jump on the line for the Log Flume, resulting in a welcome soaking and a much-needed cool-down.

We found Douglas peacefully sitting at a concession table just outside the Flume ride exit, nursing a fresh beer he purchased from a free-standing hut nearby. We grabbed a round for ourselves and joined him. Kerri pulled out a map she snatched at the entrance, and we plotted our next move.

"Hey, John, didn't you want to go on Lightning Loops?" she suggested, pointing to an area on the glossy foldout.

The Big Man looked at the map and immediately put the kibosh on the idea. "That's all the way on the other end of the fucking park. I'm not in the mood to walk all that way."

"Why don't we just take the Skyway?" Tony said, tracing a dark red line in the middle of the map. "It goes all the way to the other side and stops in front of the Lightning Loops."

The entrance to the Skyway was about 50 yards away. The gondola-style cars were initially built for the 1964 World's Fair in New York's Flushing Meadows Park and donated to Six Flags after the Fair closed. Transversing the property in about eight minutes, the cars reach a pinnacle of more than 100 feet in the air.

Douglas grabbed a fresh round of beers for everyone as we headed to the Skyway. Colquhoun, the Mooch, Mr. B, and Tony joined me in one car (breaking the four-adult limit) while Douglas and Big Man rode with Kerri and Barbara. Barely a minute into the ride and way above the pedestrian-walking crowd, we heard screams from the other gondola. Big Man was standing up, causing it to sway back and forth.

Not to be outdone, Mr. B followed suit, and soon, most of our beer found its way to the gondola floor.

Peter the Mooch reached into his pocket and produced the leftover nickel from his park admission. "See that guy in the white baseball hat and a blue tank top? Bombs Away!" And with that, he released the coin, and we watched in anticipation as it descended closer and closer to the target. It was a direct hit.

We howled with laughter and quickly hid when the guy looked up to see where the hell that projectile came from.

Not to be outdone, Mr. B grabbed his nickel and picked out a woman pushing a stroller wearing an oversized wicker sun hat. Although he had the timing, the bomb veered off to the left, missing at the last second. Mr. B let out an exasperated "FUCK!" so loud everyone on the ground looked up.

After seeing what was happening in our gondola, The Big Man shouted for us to watch his attempt from the other car. Instead of dropping a coin, he poured some of his beer over the side, drenching some poor bastard below, just minding his own business.

Arriving at Lightning Loops, we climbed the 50-foot stairway to one of the starting platforms. Two platforms perpendicular to each other dropped the rollercoaster-like cars through a set of interlocking loops until you reached the platform at the other end. I rode with Tony in the front car while Peter, Mr. B, Colquhoun, and The Big Man occupied vehicles behind us. Douglas found another kiosk selling beer and anchored himself there with Kerri and Barbara.

Initially, we dropped quickly to ground level like a roller coaster, rapidly climbing once inside the giant loop. To make it even more frightening, the cars from the other platform were deployed, so both sets of riders entered the loops simultaneously, going above and below each other. When you reached the top of the circle, you were upside down and suspended in mid-air for a few seconds, experiencing weightlessness.

Upon completing the loop, the ride continued to the rear platform, where it came to a stop. Although we were stopped cold, no attendant arrived to release us.

"Why aren't they letting us out?" Colquhoun said.

"I don't know," I said. "Maybe they have to…"

Without warning, the cars began moving again, only in reverse.

I thought I heard a muffled "Fuck me!" from the car behind us.

We were propelled backward through the interlocking loops, ending back where we started. That was it for us.

Wobbling off "Lightning Loops," we reconnected with a relaxed Douglas and the girls at the "Great American Hamburger Hut" to stuff a few burgers down our throats and head back to the Whale, knowing we still had plenty of beer to tap.

The beer was nice and cold, and we hit the keg hard with Kerri and Barbara, making friends with other tailgating Jukes fans and sharing beers with those who didn't have any. When the time came, we jumped on a courtesy tram to gain re-entry back into the park.

Our goal was to position ourselves near the entrance of the Great Arena before the Jukes took the stage. But as we approached, there was music already coming from inside. Picking up the pace, we sprinted to the chain link gates, only to find them closed. It turns out the band was going through a sound check. Although the six-foot-high privacy screen prevented us from watching, that wouldn't stop Tony and Peter.

The duo began to climb the fence to hover above the screening, which gave them a bird's-eye view of the stage at the opposite end of the arena. Unfortunately, the closed gates were not adequately coupled together. As they reached the pinnacle, their weight caused the gates to detach from each other and slowly open, leaving them hanging six feet off the ground.

The gate opened inward to the right, eventually smashing into the concrete wall. As it hit the wall, they slowly slid down like Wile E. Coyote after becoming a victim of The Road Runner.

The 7:00 show, as expected, was packed for the Jukes.

With excellent positioning on the floor, we thoroughly enjoyed the

60-minute performance. By the end, we were tired and sweaty. As you must know by now, the Jukes never disappoint. We jumped on the log flume again to cool off, but we still had more than two hours to kill before the final show.

We retreated to the Whale, continuing to party with other Jukes fans who were also killing time.

Even though we were burnt toast, we dragged our sorry asses back into the park at about 10:30. However, we got a second wind when the Jukes hit the stage at 11:00.

Since the arena wasn't nearly as inhabited as for the first show, we easily made it down to the front. By the time they got to "Havin' a Party," even Southside Johnny looked like a rag doll.

By the time the clock struck midnight, less than 100 people remained. When Southside came out for the encore, he commented, "Where the hell did everyone go?"

Barbara and Kerri yelled in unison, "We're still here!"

Southside peered directly at them and said, "Well, then. What do you want to hear?"

"I Don't Wanna Go Home!"

Southside turned around and looked at the band, then pivoted back to Barbara and Kerri, saying, "I don't want to go home either, but didn't we play that one already?"

"Play it again!"

Southside shook his head and, laughing, said, "But, but, but, I don't wanna go home!" The Jukes launched into the crowd-pleaser a second time.

It felt like a private concert.

CHAPTER 5
THE PARKING LOT NIGHTMARE

The ride back to the Whale on the courtesy tram was slow, as almost everyone leaving the park packed into the vehicles. We made about 20 stops before getting to our lot and pole 23. Thank goodness Barbara had written it down. By this time, I was shot and was sure the rest of our little group would have been no help.

That said, arriving back at the Whale gave us a second wind. Douglas was the first to the keg, loading the last bag of ice from the cooler. My brother opened the back doors and grabbed the box speakers, positioning them on the top of the White Whale. Turning on the radio, we blasted WNEW-FM into the cool evening air. The exiting traffic was horrific, so this was a much better option.

Tony found a frisbee buried under the platform, and we hung out for over an hour until the keg was officially dead, mingling with the occasional lingering Jukes fan. The parking lot was mostly empty now, so we removed the now-floating keg from the tub and dragged it to the edge of the door. Hefting one side higher than the other, we dumped out all the water. Thanks to The Professor, plenty of unmelted ice cubes remained.

That's when we realized we were the last car left. It was past 1:00 am, and it was time to button up the Whale for the long journey home.

Tony returned the speakers to their home under the platform, and we loaded our sorry asses into the Whale. I checked with my brother to confirm he was okay with driving, but he wasn't drinking during our post-concert party. If anything, he was undoubtedly the soberest person around.

With the key already in the ignition "alt" position, so we had the power to play the radio, Tony grabbed it and twisted it the rest of the way.

The Whale wouldn't start.

"Oh, fuck," he said.

As the co-pilot, my responsibility was to help navigate and ensure the pilot stayed awake. Knowing what was happening was also in my best interests, so I asked.

"Oh, fuck what?"

"It's dead."

"What's dead?"

"The car. The battery is dead."

"Are you sure?"

"Of course, I'm fucking sure. Listen…"

Pumping the gas pedal once or twice, he turned the ignition key again —nothing but an unusual clicking sound.

In retrospect, using the battery to run the stereo for an hour wasn't the wisest of decisions.

So, we exited the Whale and waited until a security car with a rotating yellow light on the top arrived to give us a jump.

We were reminded not to put additional strain on the battery, meaning no radio. At that point in the evening, we didn't have many complaints.

Tony maneuvered the mostly silent Whale out of the parking lot onto Great Adventure Boulevard, and we followed the signs with arrows pointing the way to the NJ Turnpike. Traveling on I-195, a small blue sign appeared announcing, "NJ TURNPIKE 5 MILES."

I read it to myself and started chuckling.

A stupid jingle popped into my head. It was so ridiculous that I struggled as to whether I should repeat it out loud. But I chuckled again as it went through my brain a second time. Before I knew it, I was mumbling the jingle like I was a piano player in a slow-jazz band from the South:

"Five miles to the Turnpike, don't wanna see what I look like."

I chuckled again, only this time out loud. Turning around in the passenger captain's seat, I repeated it louder this time. Now, I felt more like that guy behind the piano and exaggerated the southern pronunciation.

"Five miles to the Turnpike, don't wanna see what I look like."

I got a few giggles, but not the response I hoped for. Then Mr. B mimicked my initial prose and added a second line:

"Five miles to the Turnpike, don't wanna see what I look like. Five miles to the Turnpike. Oh, Lord, just get me home."

The Big Man pulled it all together for one definitive version, repeating both verses.

Soon, we were all crooning our new mantra:

"Five miles to the Turnpike, don't wanna see what I look like. Five miles to the turnpike. Oh, Lord, just get me home."

We were still singing as we neared the Jersey Turnpike toll plaza. Tony maneuvered the Whale close enough to snatch the small, rectangular cardboard ticket identifying where your vehicle entered the Turnpike, handing it to me for safekeeping. When exiting the turnpike, you presented it to the toll booth operator, and he knew how much to charge.

Suddenly, a strange noise emanated from the belly of the Whale. It started very low and slowly picked up volume. At first, we weren't sure what the sound was or where it was coming from.

"Wooooooooooooooooooooo."

"What the fuck is that?" I said.

Mr. B was sitting on the van's floor and leaning against the mid-engine hub.

"I think it's coming from the engine…"

CHAPTER 6
THE PROBLEM AT HAND

"Wooooooooooooooooooo."

"The engine is leaking water," Tony said, "We need to add it to the radiator. I'm gonna pull over to the side of the plaza and see if we can find some."

The "wooooo-ing" continued as he maneuvered near a utility building. Tony spotted a garden hose connected to a spigot on the wall and moved closer for a better look. Putting the car in park, he made sure not to turn off the engine.

"If we can grab that hose," he said, "We can fill the radiator without shutting off the engine."

"Get the fuck out of here," I said, giving him the Italian wave of the hand for emphasis. "Let me get this straight: you're going to open the freakin' cap while the engine is running, and it won't explode?"

"It will not explode," he said matter-of-factly. "I've done it before."

"He's right," offered the Professor, disguised as Douglas, lying on the bed with his eyes closed but coherent enough to add to the conversation. "I do it all the time, too."

This I gotta see.

"Wooooooooooo," the Whale continued, singing a little louder.

Tony and The Big Man ventured out, confirming the spigot was operational with a quick turn of the handle. Tony returned to the Whale, dragging the orange industrial-sized hose through the open side doors. The Big Man waited for the signal to start the water flowing.

With the engine still running, Tony opened the access hood between the driver and passenger seats, allowing the "wooooooooo-ing" to escape at top volume.

Grabbing a rag stashed under the driver's seat and wrapping it around his hand, he reached in to twist the cap. Mr. B and I closed our eyes and turned our backs, afraid to witness the expected violent eruption not unlike "Old Faithful."

But nothing happened, just like Tony and the Professor promised.

Tony shoved the open end of the orange hose down the Whale's esophagus like a surgeon placing a breathing tube into a patient and signaled for Big Man to turn on the water. The rushing liquid soon silenced the Whale. Once full, Tony signaled The Big Man to turn off the water and replaced the cap.

"While the car is running," he said, showing us where he added the precious fluid like an Auto-Shop teacher, "you have back pressure, and the liquid is cycling through the engine. That's why it doesn't blow up when you open the cap."

As accurate as that statement might have been, we had a much larger problem on our hands.

"We're okay for now, but this is only going to work for about a half-hour or so," Tony said, "There's a leak somewhere that we can't repair ourselves. When it gets below a certain level, it's going to make that wooooo-ing sound. That's our clue to refill the tank."

"And how do you propose we do that?" I asked.

"Well, I just showed you we can add water directly into the radiator without stopping the engine," he said.

"Let's see if they have some containers we can use."

Mr. B suggested using the empty keg tub as a repository. Tony's eyes lit up, and he signaled for The Big Man to turn on the water again. He promptly filled the basin about halfway. Topping off the radiator again before returning the hose, we settled uneasily back into the Whale for the long trip up the Jersey Turnpike, not knowing if we would make it.

We had been back on the road for about 20 minutes or so, and all was quiet. Peter and Douglas were dead asleep on the makeshift bed while John Colquhoun passed out, slumped against the side wall. If he were one of his cartoon characters, giant "ZZZZZ's" would be in a bubble above his head. The Big Man was again positioned atop the cooler, snoring loudly. Mr. B was still on the floor, leaning on the engine compartment and trying to keep me awake in the passenger seat.

"Wooooooooooooo."

Mr. B sprang into action, grabbing an empty cup and filling it with water. I slid into the back of the van and opened the cover. The "woooo-ing" sound was low but starting to crescendo. I wrapped the rag around my hand and twisted the radiator cap, fully expecting an explosion of steam. Of course, as Tony and Douglas predicted, nothing happened. Mr. B adeptly poured five or six cups into the belly of the Whale until the ungodly noise stopped and added one more for good luck. We continued on our way.

"Wooooooooooooo."

Only Tony was conscious when the Whale's digestive system called for water again. I was in La-La-Land when he reached over and smacked me in the head.

"Aren't you supposed to be awake?"

I mumbled about resting my eyes, but I was startled awake by the "Woooooo-ing," approaching a much higher decibel. Everyone was up now.

"Somebody fix that fucking thing," the Mooch yelled from the back.

Mr. B and I sprang into action, soothing the savage beast with water and shutting down the steam whistle.

Most of them had fallen asleep again, and I tried to stay engaged with Tony as he drove. But as I was about to doze off again…

"Wooooooooooooooo" emanated from the back of the van. Only it wasn't coming from the engine; it was coming from Peter the Mooch.

"Wooooooooooooo," he mimicked, much to the delight of everyone in the back, who began to throw small, unsecured items in his general direction to shut him up.

After a few minutes of silence, Mr. B joined the mimicking. This nonsense would continue for the remainder of the ride home.

In between fake "wooooos" and actual "wooooos" requiring the addition of water into the radiator, we made it out of New Jersey, through Staten Island, across the Verrazzano Bridge, and into Brooklyn. When we got to the Belt Parkway, it was close to 4:00 am, and everyone was dead asleep except for Tony.

CHAPTER 7
THE LAST GASP

Tony guided the Whale into a gas station positioned on the median between the east and westbound traffic on the Belt, near Coney Island. Maneuvering near the pump, he shut off the engine as the attendant approached the vehicle. Once the tank was filled, Tony planned on adding more water to the radiator before we left, hoping to complete the trip home without any additional "woooooo-ing." He sat in the driver's seat while the attendant did the pumping.

Then the sun came up.

My brother woke up with his head planted on the steering wheel. He was sleeping so soundly that he wasn't sure where he was. Only snoring was emanating from the back of the van. It was after 6:00 am. We had been anchored at the gas station for over two hours but were still parked at the pump we initially pulled up to.

Tony gathered his senses and entered the small building where the attendant hid while waiting for customers.

"What happened?" Tony asked.

"You fell asleep while I was pumping the gas," the attendant replied.

"Why didn't you wake me up?"

"We can't. It's against the law. We have to let you sleep it off."

"Right next to the pump?"

"Yes, sir."

Tony paid the dude and slipped back into the driver-side seat. Saying a little prayer under his breath and turning the ignition key, the Whale sprang to life. He whacked me on the head to snap me awake and tell me what happened.

"Well," I said, "At least you got some shuteye."

After refilling the Whale's water tank and resuming co-pilot duties, I stayed conscious the rest of the way and did everything possible to ensure Tony did so, too. Everyone else passed out dead in the back, including Mr. B.

"Well, this was an interesting road trip, huh?" I said to Tony.

"It looks like it was a good thing we had that keg, especially the tub," he said. "I don't know how we would have made it home without it."

We quietly navigated onto the Southern State Parkway and were now just a few exits from Massapequa.

"If I never hear that fucking wooooo-ing again," I said, "It will be too soon."

"I gotta get that fixed today," he said, "Well, maybe tomorrow."

Tony pulled the Whale off Exit 30 and into Massapequa. Just then, as if on cue, we heard it again.

"Woooooooooooooo."

Only this time, it was coming from Peter the Mooch.

He picked up his head and flashed his bloodshot eyes with a big smile.

"Go fuck yourself, man," I told him…

PART SIX

MEETING ACROSS THE RIVER

The Night Matty Almost Bled to Death

(February 1982)

PROLOGUE

I wondered if this day would ever end.

Don't get me wrong; I was proud to have a "real" job instead of being a college graduate still working at the mall. Besides being the "Shoe Guy" at a junior sportswear store called Pants Place Plus, I also worked a part-time gig as an editorial assistant at Long Island's newspaper, *Newsday*. As it turned out, my rudimentary computer work at *Newsday* inadvertently helped me obtain a position at Goldwater Hospital, part of the New York City Health and Hospital Corporation.

In 1980, my friend Bruce (Mr. B) had a job interview at Goldwater, located on Roosevelt Island in the middle of the East River. Russ Dower, the chain-smoking father of our friends Doug, Barbara, and Susan, was the comptroller at the time. They sought to hire someone to work with the software vendor SMS (Shared Medical Systems) to install a new long-term care system and thought Bruce might be interested in the job. Goldwater housed almost 2,000 long-term care patients.

Since Manhattan could be accessed via the Roosevelt Island tram, I'd planned to tag along, say hello to Mr. Dower, and travel across the East River. I'd lined up several interviews with magazines later in the afternoon and would hop on the Long Island Railroad back home.

Mr. Dower introduced us to Mark Kator, the CFO. Mark and I were alone while Bruce was being interviewed, discussing how technology was changing business operations. We talked about my work at *Newsday* and how reporters were using an electronic word processor, replacing the need for manual typewriters and paper. I monitored the computer and moved files electronically from the writer's queue to the editors. Mark asked about my interest in becoming a newspaper reporter someday. I explained how *Newsday*, unfortunately, only hired writers with two or more years of experience with a daily newspaper.

After Bruce finished, we said our goodbyes to Mr. Dower and Mark, did a quick doobie in the back parking lot, and went our separate ways. Bruce's interview was a formality, as he already had the job. Despite the disaster a few years earlier during Super Bowl weekend in Pennsylvania, Mr. Dower always liked him and thought he was an upstanding citizen.

Obviously, he was more familiar with Bruce's genial "Eddie Haskel" personality and not his alter-ego, Mr. B.

Later that evening, while working at *Newsday* and answering the phones, an unfamiliar voice asked to speak with Paul DiSclafani. It turned out to be Mr. Dower. He wanted to offer me the job at Goldwater.

I respectfully declined, letting him know I couldn't do that to Bruce.

"No, you asshole," he said, "I want to hire both of you."

I told him about my *Newsday* position and my hope to be a reporter someday, and I would like to consider his offer.

"Well, if you change your mind, it pays $12,500 a year with 12 holidays, four weeks of vacation, three personal days, and 12 sick days."

I thought about it for five seconds and then took the job. I barely made enough money at *Newsday* and my job in the mall to cover my beer and girlfriend expenses (whom I eventually married) and needed cash.

Thus, my lifetime employment as a Healthcare IT Professional began.

Of course, I didn't have to enjoy my work at the time…

CHAPTER 1
THE PLAN

"If I have to sign one more fucking Claim Form-B, I'm going to kill someone," I declared to no one in particular.

The Patient Accounting Department needed to manually review and sign over 1,500 Medicaid Claim Form-B bills twice a month. That's a shitload of claims processed and sent out every two weeks.

Looking at the clock again, I wondered if the hands were moving.

I caught Mr. B smiling and happily working his share of the mountainous pile of those little green and white forms.

"Patience, my friend," he said. "Wanna step out for the pause that refreshes?"

That question never required an answer.

Goldwater Hospital stood on the southern tip of Roosevelt Island, which was nestled in the East River between Manhattan and Queens, underneath the shadow of the Queensboro Bridge. The hospital faced Manhattan and offered a spectacular view of the United Nations. We would often grab our friend Edgar from across the hall in Medical Records to smoke a doobie. Most of our coworkers were around the same age and enjoyed the occasional pause that refreshes.

It was late February 1982, and my 25th birthday was coming the following week. Although nature provided us an unseasonably warm day, the temperature dropped with the limited sunshine. Being on an island wasn't helping. I grabbed my parka from the closet and headed out. Leaning on the railing facing Manhattan, Mr. B fired up a joint as the three of us stared blankly across the water.

"Did you hear back from Big Man?" I asked Mr. B.

Taking a hit, he held it briefly, then exhaled. "Yep, he's in, and so is Matty. Did you hear from Colquhoun?"

"He told me he would try to make it," I said through closed lips after inhaling, trying not to let too much smoke escape. "He's not far from Penn. He lives on Fourteenth and Eighth." Exhaling, I turned to hand the joint to Edgar. "What about you, Edgar? Wanna join us for a pre-birthday celebration?"

"Nah," he said as he took his turn. "You guys are too wild for me. I've got a nice, mellow weekend planned with my girl."

"Bochicchio is in, right?" I asked Mr. B.

With his lungs filled with smoke, he shook his head in the affirmative.

Bob Bochicchio (left) and Mr. B (right) at my wedding in 1983.

Our introduction to Bob Bochicchio came while working at Goldwater after he transferred into Patient Accounts from Finance, and we hit it off immediately. He was always impeccably dressed. His curly hair was neatly cropped, and he sported a classic, pencil-thin,

'80s-style mustache. We affectionately called him "Uncle Bob." He was (and still is) one of the funniest people I have ever met, with a wonderful, dry sense of humor.

What started as a couple of guys meeting across the river in Manhattan for dinner and a few adult beverages would quickly turn into an evening of debauchery. Our friend Kevin (whom everyone called Slim) shared an apartment with Mr. B and me in Flushing, so he didn't need much convincing.

Uncle Bob was already on board. The Big Man, our friend Matty, and John Colquhoun also decided to join us. Our first stop would be Beefsteak Charlies at Penn Station.

Bruce and Kevin developed a friendship as co-workers at the Dime Savings Bank in the Sunrise Mall. Bruce also knew Matty from around the neighborhood in Massapequa Park, where they lived a few blocks from each other. I met Matty in high school. John Colquhoun became friends with us while at the student newspaper at New York Tech and was turning into a world-class illustrator.

Matty would jump on the train from Rockville Centre, where he worked for a pharmaceutical company called Darby. The Big Man and Slim worked downtown in the Financial District and would take the subway to Penn. Colquhoun, who lived in the city on Fourteenth Street, would hoof the 20 or so blocks uptown.

Roosevelt Island did not have subway service. The only ways on and off the island were by car using a small bridge on 36th Avenue in Astoria or by tram from Manhattan. The tram traversed the East River parallel to the Queensboro Bridge, dropping passengers on the other side at 59th Street and Second Avenue in seven minutes. Goldwater was a short walk from the tram.

Unless you lived in Manhattan, most drove to work on Roosevelt Island via the 36th Avenue bridge from Astoria. Bruce and I had a short commute from our apartment in Flushing while Uncle Bob still traveled from his parent's home on Long Island in West Hempstead.

We would rendezvous at 6:00.

Seven guys meeting for dinner at Beefsteak Charlie's, the only place in town with an all-you-can-eat shrimp and salad bar. Did I mention they served unlimited beer, wine, and sangria?

What could possibly go wrong?

CHAPTER 2
THE DEBACLE AT BEEFSTEAK CHARLIE'S

As soon as the clock struck 5:00, Uncle Bob, Mr. B, and I headed to my car, parked behind the hospital in the employee lot overlooking Queens, for a beer and a joint. Bob arrived later than usual that day, forcing him to park at the remote southern tip of the lot, far from the employee entrance. Mine was more conveniently located.

I loaded a six-pack and some ice that morning in my trusty red cooler. After work, we knocked back a few with Uncle Bob, then drove around the loop to the front of the hospital where all the muckety-mucks had reserved parking spots during business hours. However, after hours, anyone could park there. This would save time when we returned; besides, there was no decent lighting in the back.

Securing a primo spot, we walked to the tram.

The Manhattan and Roosevelt Island bound trams ran consecutively every 7-10 minutes, side by side in opposite directions. The crossing took about seven minutes, and the cable cars would pass each other about 300 feet above the East River. A ride on the tram cost the same as a subway token, but the view was spectacular, especially at night.

After touching down on Second Avenue, we hailed a cab for Penn Station. Upon arriving, we found The Big Man and Slim were already seated comfortably at the bar inside Beefsteak Charlie's, so we joined them for a drink. Colquhoun and Matty would arrive shortly.

As far as anyone knew, we were a smartly dressed group of young businessmen. Uncle Bob, who always wore a suit and tie, spent time with Bruce and me to help us look more professional. We never wore suits (only ties), but he taught us how to make a proper knot.

Both Slim and The Big Man were also dressed in suits every day. Slim, who worked at a brokerage house, wore very expensive suits. I remember telling him about a place in the Mall I found selling three neckties for $10. He just laughed and shook his head.

"Disco, this is a $300 suit. You think I'm going to wear a $3 tie?"

Colquhoun was the only member of our entourage without a tie. He was more of a casual, artistic type. However, he looked cool in his collared red and blue striped Rugby shirt.

With our band of Merrymen accounted for, Uncle Bob signaled to the pretty hostess that we were ready. She grabbed a handful of menus and flashed her pearly whites. "Follow me, please!"

She led us to a table conveniently located near the salad and shrimp bar. After taking our seats, she handed us menus before turning tail and heading back to the main entrance for the next group. And what a tail she possessed.

A tall waiter wearing a white shirt, black vest, and a bow tie greeted us immediately. Before he could say, "Good evening," we ordered seven pitchers of their finest watered-down beer.

Mr. B grabbed me by the shoulders and pointed to the waiter. "It's my friend's birthday, my good man. Keep those pitchers coming!"

He returned quickly with the 24 oz plastic pitchers (we didn't need glasses), and we all stood to toast my 25th birthday. We reached across the table to clink our pitchers while yelling, "Salude!" or "Nastrovia!" Instead of the magical "clinking" sound you expect with delicate glassware, there was only a dull thud.

We stacked the empties on each other, assembling a reasonable facsimile of the Leaning Tower of Pisa. Our server remained on top of things, bless his little heart, retrieving the empties and returning with full ones. I can't even begin calculating how many empty pitchers we accumulated. After hitting the shrimp and salad bar, we ordered the usual Charlie's dinner—steak and a baked potato for $9.99.

By the time we finished, the surface of our table resembled a feast during the Roman Empire, with carnage everywhere. Shrimp carcasses decorated the floor like discarded peanut shells. Half-eaten steak sat on lonely plates, and any unfinished baked potato got rewrapped in aluminum foil and used as small footballs to be tossed across the room whenever someone got up to pee.

The Big Man decided to up the ante. Procuring one of the uneaten crustaceans, he waved it in front of my face and pointed to the buffet table about 20 feet away. "You think I could land this shrimp back in the bowl from here?"

"From here? Anyone could do that," I said. "Try launching it with a fork, like a catapult. Now, that would be something to see."

We cleared some space in the rubble to position our forks and loaded them with one of the little buggers. Slim caught on to our experiment and yelled, "Fire in the hole!"

The extended open buffet area contained the salad and fixings, anchored on both ends with giant shrimp bowls. Although we achieved enough height using the fork catapult, we couldn't get enough distance, and the tiny crustaceans would invariably land on some unexpected diner's head. It didn't take long for the other patrons to figure out who was launching shrimp into the air like ballistic missiles.

We managed to pay the bill (leaving a hefty 10% tip, I might add) and stepped out into the crisp night. Unfortunately, we had no plan other than meeting at Beefsteak Charlie's and drinking as much beer as possible in about an hour.

"You guys want to head uptown?" Slim asked. "I went to this place once in the theatre district that was kind of cool."

"Sure, why not?" said Mr. B. "Let's stop at a deli for beer."

After all, we needed to head back to 59th Street anyway to grab the tram since my car and Uncle Bob's were back at the hospital on Roosevelt Island. Colquhoun already lived in Manhattan, but Big Man and Matty would be taking the Long Island Railroad home.

What a great idea! More beer before we head to another bar.

CHAPTER 3
THE TREK UPTOWN

I met John Colquhoun at New York Tech while working on the school newspaper, and we became good friends. A talented illustrator, he was also the editor of *The Campus Slate*, which ran our weekly Team FUBAR "Brewing Out" column. He had been on several adventures with us and knew Bruce and The Big Man from New York Tech.

One night, we got together for an evening of debauchery at our apartment in Flushing with our friend, George Savold, whom we have called "The Sav" since high school. The Sav and Colquhoun joined Mr. B and me on a trip to The Assembly, a bar in Bayside.

In addition to a cool-looking interior restaurant, The Assembly boasted a great outdoor seating area with a separate bar and bartender. We headed there for a nightcap, occupying stools at the bar. We were the only people outside this late in the evening.

After a few beers, the barkeep asked where we were from. When we told him we were originally from Long Island, he asked if we ever drank a Long Island Iced Tea. We were beer drinkers, so hard liquor was not usually in our limited budgets.

"Have at it, my man!" I said.

He mixed up enough for four drinks.

They were so good; we had another, then another, then another.

As the night progressed, we were getting increasingly wasted, and so was our new drink-pouring friend, who apparently wasn't taking the "don't drink with the patrons" rule of thumb seriously. Finally, he said, "Hey, I don't even know your names. I'm Pete."

Thinking it would be better to offer our given names instead of our nicknames, I reached out and shook his hand. "Pleasure to meet you, Pete. I'm Paul."

I pointed to Colquhoun and said, "This is my friend, John."

As Colquhoun waved, I pointed to The Sav and said, "This is my other friend, George."

Suddenly, Bill smiled as he reached out his hand to Mr. B before I could complete the introductions. "Let me guess—you must be Ringo?"

Back to our story.

The fresh, cool air sobered me up as we made the trek uptown. I can't say the same for the others, but with how they acted, the beer we drank at Beefsteak Charlie's wouldn't dissipate too soon. We headed into a deli along Seventh Avenue and picked up some tall boys for the walk, strategically placing them into our coat pockets for safekeeping (and quick access). Nobody wanted to be walking around with paper bags, you know.

We popped into a small bar during the closing moments of Happy Hour, ordered a few drinks, and played pool. I wasn't in the mood for beer, so I ordered shots of Jack Daniels for the group. Matty jumped in and took things to the next level, calling for the Jack to be topped off with Peppermint Schnapps. Back in Massapequa, at our home base of Jocelyn's, we called that a "snowshoe." The schnapps increased the potency and helped soften the Jack's bite.

We hung out until Happy Hour concluded, gathered ourselves, and continued on our way. The temperature dropped considerably, but it did not affect our ability to walk as much as the multiple shots of Jack.

Rosie O'Grady's was a massive establishment on the corner of Seventh Avenue and 52nd Street. A glowing "T" shaped neon red sign on the building could be seen from a few blocks away. The letters spelling out ROSIE were brightly lit across the top, but some letters forming the word "O'GRADY," which ran down the stem of the "T," were unlit. In the dark, the sign read ROSIE OGRY.

"Thar, she blows!" Matty yelled, pointing to the beckoning neon.

"Does that say Rosie's Orgy?" I inquired.

"I hope so," Uncle Bob chimed in.

CHAPTER 4
THE INCIDENT

Rosie O'Grady's featured a vast restaurant with many tables. It certainly didn't look and feel like a bar. Slim pointed to the staircase in the middle of the floor, to the left of the entrance. "The bar is downstairs."

The double-wide stairs contained a handrail in the center. We took our cue and followed Slim down to Rosie's Pub.

Significantly smaller than the dining area upstairs, the Pub was smartly configured and populated with quite a few people in the common areas. People nursing drinks surrounded the high-top bistro tables while others, seated at regular tables, ordered food with a server.

A bar with rounded corners ran almost the entire length of the downstairs wall. We made our way down to the far end of the bar and took residence there. The barback was covered in mirrors and glass shelves filled with different-shaped bottles. I wondered who actually drinks that crap?

The last place we needed to be was another bar. It had been a long evening of drinking, but it was still early. Many beers were on tap, which meshed well with the beer we drank all night. Unlike the pitchers we got at Beefsteak Charlies, Rosie's only served tap beer in single-serve mugs.

The bartender reached into the freezer and grabbed a handful of those old-fashioned, heavy glass mugs with oversized handles on the sides. The beer stayed cold in those frosty mugs, but because the glass was thick, they probably held about 10 oz instead of the 12 typically found in a bottle. On the other hand, the mugs were significantly cheaper, so what's a few ounces between friends?

Considering our current inebriated state, we were the loudest patrons in good ole' Rosie's Pub. Although we did not stumble or knock things over, we were making a general nuisance of ourselves. We were yelling at the TV while the Knicks were playing and loudly calling to each other.

The Big Man, Matty, and I faced each other at the bar's curved end. Deep into their conversation, Mr. B, Slim, and Uncle Bob surrounded and commandeered one of the high-top bistro tables. Colquhoun was wandering around before stopping and becoming transfixed by a picture of the New York City skyline at night attached to the wall behind Mr. B.

Matty Wynn

Meanwhile, Matty was waving his hands, trying to attract the bartender's attention and yelling for him to bring us some shots of Jack and Peppermint Schnapps. After making eye contact, the bartender grabbed a towel to wipe his wet hands and headed toward us.

Colquhoun maneuvered closer to the picture and pulled a Swiss army knife from his pocket. Blindly locating the Phillips head screwdriver attachment, he unscrewed one of the fasteners securing the artwork to the wall.

Back at the bar, Matty tried explaining the snowshoe ingredients to the bartender, who wasn't grasping the concept.

"So, you want two shots?" he asked for clarity, tilting his head slightly to the left.

"No. It's a shot of Jack topped off with Peppermint Schnapps in the same glass."

"If I do that, I'm gonna have to charge you for two shots."

Matty, who has also bartended at times, shook his head back and forth. "No fucking way. It's a partial shot of Jack with Schnapps as a top-off. It makes one full shot. What don't you understand about that?"

As the bartender was about to answer, he caught a glimpse over Matty's shoulder of Colquhoun working feverishly to remove another screw from the picture.

"Hey! What the fuck do you think you're doing?" he said loud enough to turn the heads of the general population in the bar.

Turning calmly to face him, Colquhoun responded, "I thought I would like to take this home, sir. I like the way it…."

"Stop that right now, or I'll have you thrown out. Am I making myself clear?"

Just then, two bouncers started moving toward Colquhoun.

Matty tapped his empty beer mug on the surface of the bar a few times in an attempt to refocus the bartender's attention.

"Hey, you gettin' me those shots, or what?"

From behind Matty, Mr. B chimed in, "Yeah, man! We need those shots. We're celebrating a birthday, man. This is bullshit!"

The bartender turned to Matty with fire in his eyes. "Are you fucking kidding me? All right, that's it. You guys are done. Grab your shit, leave the fucking picture on the wall, and get your asses out of here!"

Ever the diplomat, I attempted to reason with him to no avail.

"Look, man," I said, "I apologize for these guys. We'll behave." I pointed to Colquhoun, who was reattaching the frame. "See? The picture is back on the wall. Can't you give us one more round, and we'll be out of here."

The bartender turned to me. "Hey, asshole, did you not hear me? Get the fuck out now, or I will have all of you thrown out on your asses!"

There wasn't much room to negotiate at this point, and it was in our best interests to head upstairs and out the door.

But Matty was having none of it.

"This is fucked," he said.

Not one to take no for an answer, Matty picked up his mug again, only this time he smashed it hard onto the bar top, shattering the heavy glass into fragments. At that exact moment, I saw the rage in Matty's eyes and swiveled on my barstool to cover my head, turning my back to him.

"Nobody cuts us off!" he declared, except now only the curved mug handle remained in his right hand. The rest of it was gone.

Unfortunately, one end of the broken handle was now jutting into his wrist. Instinctively, Matty removed the broken glass and stared as blood began spurting out with every heartbeat.

Now what?

CHAPTER 5
THE EMERGENCY ROOM DEBACLE

Blood was shooting everywhere by now.

Matty stood up and turned to Mr. B and Slim, splashing them with his heart-pumped blood. Sitting next to Matty, The Big Man had red streaks across his chest. The bartender froze in fear as the Matty fountain continued to spurt.

Reaching for Matty's wrist, I was squirted with O-negative on my shirt and blue striped tie. Although my first thought was, "There goes a good $3 tie," I slapped my hand over the vein to apply pressure and led him up the stairs and to a bustling Seventh Avenue. Holding Matty's wrist over his head, we stood in front of Rosie O'Grady's, waiting for the others to join us after grabbing the coats and paying our tab.

Matty told me he didn't need my help to keep the pressure on his wrist. I removed my hand so he could view the wound. The cut was deep, and the blood had momentarily stopped spurting. But in the next heartbeat, it shot out again, streaming onto the hood of a white Volkswagen parked out front. Matty froze, watching as the blood continued to spurt rhythmically. Bump-Bump. Bump-Bump. With every other "bump," Old Faithful would go off, spraying in different directions. Matty's wrist was beginning to resemble an impact sprinkler used for watering lawns. Only the water coming from this sprinkler was crimson red. The Volkswagen and the sidewalk now resembled a crime scene following a mobster rubout.

He looked at me, and I at him. After two or three more spurts, I clamped my hand over his wrist again and said, "We better get out of here right now."

With the remaining inebriated and frightened crew joining us on the street level, I turned to Mr. B. "This is bad. We gotta get him to a hospital."

An FDNY firetruck crossed 53rd Street as if on cue, so Mr. B and The Big Man ran down there to ask for help. They recommended we keep applying pressure and walk to St. Claire's Hospital, only two blocks away on 51st and Ninth Avenue. Taking turns putting pressure on Matty's wrist, we kept it elevated on the trek to St. Claire's. Each time we switched, another spurt of blood would escape.

One of the oldest hospitals in the city and located in a residential neighborhood, St. Claire's, unlike modern healthcare facilities, avoided bright lights or signage. At no time could the word modern be used to describe anything in the facility. Situated in Manhattan's famed "Hell's Kitchen," the entrance to the hospital blended with the surrounding apartment buildings, modestly lit with a blue awning over the front door. I guess the giant white statue depicting St. Claire on the top of the canopy might be a dead giveaway, but who ever heard of St. Claire?

A nurse quickly escorted Matty into the tiny Emergency room while a registrar handed me a clipboard and asked if we could help fill out some paperwork. We gathered at a small table to see how many blanks we could fill in and realized that both Slim and Colquhoun weren't in the emergency room with us.

"Where's Slim?" asked Mr. B.

"I thought he was with you?" Uncle Bob said.

"With me? Aren't we all together?"

I looked around and couldn't find Colquhoun. "Where the hell did they go?"

Big Man poked his head out the door and found Slim walking down the block. He waved to him and returned inside. "Slim's coming down the block, but I don't see Colquhoun."

When the ER's sliding doors magically opened, Slim sashayed in, holding a tall can of beer sticking out over a way-too-short paper bag. A security guard intercepted him, stopping him in his tracks.

"Whoa, buddy," he said. "You can't come in here with that."

Slim stared at his unfinished beer, held it up to the guard as if to salute him, turned around, and went outside.

A few minutes later, he showed up on the other side of the waiting room, entering from the back of the ER. He ventured around the building to the main hospital entrance and snaked his way back into the ER from the inside. The guard approached Slim while he was still holding that same can of beer. He grabbed him by the shoulders and pointed him toward the exit. "You have to be the stupidest person I have ever seen," then bodily removed him from the room and tossed him back onto the street.

With Matty being treated, there was nothing to do but wait. Instead, we headed outside to find Slim leaning against the building's brick façade, mindlessly drinking his tall boy from a paper bag.

"Where did you get a beer?" Mr. B asked.

A small bodega sat a few hundred feet from the Emergency Room. We strolled in and found the beer refrigerator. I grabbed a handful of Tallboys while The Big Man went down the munch aisle and picked some pretzels. Uncle Bob made the rational choice and decided on a Pepsi.

I turned to Slim and asked him what happened to Colquhoun.

"I have no idea," he said. "I think he went home." Nobody could confirm whether he carried a giant picture with him.

I placed all the items on the counter and asked the clerk to put the beers in small paper bags. Instead of answering, he stared at me with horror in his eyes.

"Is there something wrong?" I asked.

"Nothing. Nothing's wrong, sir," he said, shakily ringing up the purchases. Several other people in the bodega were simultaneously staring at us while slowly inching away and keeping their distance.

I eyed the Big Man and noticed the long, red streaks of blood across his shirt. Mr. B, Slim, and Uncle Bob also contained varying bright red stains on their clothes. I checked my hands, which were covered in dried blood, as was my shirt and tie. We were a group of sharply dressed men covered in blood.

We walked back down to St. Claire's in stunned silence. Somehow, we hadn't noticed all the blood before.

Finishing our beers outside, we strolled back into the ER and headed for the bathrooms. After taking care of business, we washed the blood off our hands and arms. There was not much we could do about our clothes.

Inside, things were getting testy between Matty and the staff.

"You cahn't leave," the nurse with a Jamaican accent said while trailing Matty as he emerged from the treatment area into the waiting room.

"I am leaving," Matty said.

Staying overnight at St. Claire's was not an option in his mind. He wanted to go to a Long Island Hospital. The physician informed Matty that he needed surgery. The best they could do was a few temporary stitches to stop the bleeding if he insisted on leaving.

"Let's do that and get me the hell out of here."

Matty agreed and returned to the treatment room. They stitched Matty's wound, and he emerged with a pristine white bandage surrounding his wrist and found us in the waiting room.

"Let's go, boys," he said with the nurse trailing behind him.

"If you leave, Mr. Matt, you die," warned the nurse.

"Listen, you guys are speaking seven different languages, and I don't know any of them. I'm leaving."

We grabbed our stuff and headed out the door. Big Man was the last to leave and asked the nurse, "Is he really going to die?"

"Oh, yes, he will bleed out if doze stitches break."

CHAPTER 6
THE NEW PLAN

We needed to hatch a new plan to expeditiously transport Matty safely back to Long Island and the hospital of his choice.

Uncle Bob, who lived in West Hempstead, offered to drive Matty and Big Man instead of letting them take their chances on the Long Island Railroad. Matty wanted to be treated at Brunswick Hospital in Amityville, east of his parent's home in Massapequa. Although his car stood in Rockville Centre, Matty would deal with his transportation issues another time.

"We can't walk with Matty all the way back to the tram," Uncle Bob said, "We better grab a cab and go straight to my car on Roosevelt Island."

Try as he might, Uncle Bob could not convince Matty to go to Bellevue Hospital, a few minutes away from St. Claire's. "They have some of the best neurosurgeons in the country," Uncle Bob pleaded.

"I don't care. I'm not staying in this fucking shithole of a city."

It was a little after 11:00 pm when we said our goodbyes and wished them luck, vowing to call each other tomorrow morning to see how it turned out. Mr. B, Slim, and I headed for the E train at 50th and Eighth Avenue, which would take us to Lexington and 53rd. We could easily walk to the tram from there. The impromptu rescue party hailed a cab and disappeared into the night.

"Do you think it's safe to take the subway at this time of night?" I asked Mr. B.

Before he answered, Slim jumped in and said, "Do you think anyone is going to mess with us when our clothes are filled with blood?"

Point taken.

We found a bench in the station, ironically sitting under the sign with a giant arrow showing the way to St. Claire's Hospital. We waited almost 20 minutes for the next train. I might have dozed off, but when I heard the train pull in, I shook the other two awake, or we would have missed it.

It was a quiet and uneventful walk to the tram. Taking in the brisk air in the much colder evening woke me up, and I felt a little better. Considering we still had to drive from Roosevelt Island to Flushing, I hoped there wouldn't be any more adventures.

After mostly ignoring the majestic Manhattan views the tram provided, we dragged our sorry asses back to Goldwater, reaching my car in front of the hospital sometime after midnight. With a slightly foggy head and on auto-pilot, I maneuvered around the one-way road circling Goldwater to the back lot on the Queen's side, eventually leading through town and off the island via the 36th Avenue Bridge.

Following the one-way loop around the hospital, we passed what looked like Uncle Bob's Toyota Celica in the darkness. "Wasn't that Bob's car?"

"Nah, no way. They left over an hour ago. It's only a ten-minute ride by taxi, fifteen tops at this time of night," Mr. B said, lighting up the tip of a half-smoked joint he found in the ashtray. Slim produced a spare tall boy from his pocket. "Might as well enjoy the rest of the evening."

So, we did.

Unfortunately, as it turned out, that was Uncle Bob's car.

CHAPTER 7
THE TAXI FIASCO

After hailing the taxi, Uncle Bob directed the driver to head for the Queensboro Bridge, which would take them quickly across the river, into Astoria, and to the 36th Avenue bridge.

They never made it, as the cab blew a tire somewhere in the middle of the bridge.

"What the fuck?" cried Big Man when he felt the vibration before the cabbie pulled over to the side of the bridge. "Did you just blow a fucking tire?"

"Yes, yes," the Arab-accented driver said.

"Can you call us another cab," said Uncle Bob. "We have to get this man to a hospital right away."

"Yes, yes," the driver said. "I call for cab after you pay me fare on the meter."

"Are you out of your fucking mind?" a still slightly sedated Matty said. "We're not paying you anything. Call for another cab right now, or I'll lose my fucking mind."

The Big Man opened the back door and peered menacing into the driver's half-open window. "If you don't make that call, I'll make it for you."

"No way, no way," the cabbie insisted. "You owe me money on meter. Pay me money, I get you cab."

Matty started to lose it. He began gestating with his injured hand. "This is fucking insane!" he said. "What are we supposed to do?"

"I have spare, I have spare," the driver said, trying to exit the vehicle, but The Big Man was blocking his way.

"You better have a spare."

Big Man and Uncle Bob followed him to the back, where he grabbed the funky-looking tire from the trunk and leaned it on the driver's side of the taxi near the flat tire. That's when Matty joined them at the rear, holding up his bandaged wrist, revealing the rapidly seeping intrusion of red patterns spoiling the original snow-white covering.

Our heroes had been arguing with the cabbie for about a half hour and were far from getting onto Roosevelt Island.

Taking things into his own hands, Big Man tried to flag down random cars on the bridge, to no avail. Apparently, motorists were not prone to stopping their vehicles on the span of the Queensboro Bridge when being flagged down by a giant of a man sporting a blood-soaked suit.

The cabbie removed the flat tire from the axle and mounted the spare in its place. Our heroes, who were mindlessly leaning over the railing, contemplating how far down Roosevelt Island, directly below them might be, began to cheer. Triumphantly, he lowered the jack, revealing that the spare was also flat. Several words that were perceived to be curses spewed from his mouth in a foreign language.

Spotting a taxi in the distance with its fare light on, Big Man blocked its path, forcing it to stop and signaling for it to pull over. He obliged, maneuvering in front of their disabled cab and getting out to speak with the driver. Meanwhile, Matty's bandage was turning into a bloody mess.

They convinced the new cabbie that this was an emergency, and he agreed to take them to Roosevelt Island. Throwing the other driver five bucks for his troubles, they took off.

Back at Goldwater and safely in Bob's car, Matty said he felt woozy. His once-white bandage had turned completely red, and now it was leaking. Uncle Bob put the pedal to the metal and never stopped once, racing along the Grand Central Parkway at about 90 mph. Matty originally wanted to go to Brunswick Hospital, but it was too far away. Big Man suggested Nassau County Medical Center, but Bob said, "I wouldn't go there if I were already dead."

Instead, they headed to Long Island Jewish in New Hyde Park, less than 20 miles from Roosevelt Island and just across the Queens / Nassau border. But in their haste, they sped right past the exit without realizing they missed it.

So, they continued to Nassau County Medical Center in Uniondale (about another 12 miles farther east), even though Matty wasn't quite dead yet.

Matty was seen immediately, and the doctor confirmed the diagnosis he received back at St. Claire's. He needed emergency surgery on the damaged wrist to repair the torn ulna nerve. Uncle Bob and The Big Man stayed until they admitted him, visiting for a few minutes in the ER before they began prepping him for surgery.

"You have to call my parents and tell them I'm here," Matty instructed The Big Man. His parents had just returned from a Florida vacation earlier in the evening.

"What do you want me to tell them? I'm not crazy about lying to your father."

"I don't give a shit what you tell them; just don't tell them what really happened."

"Don't you think we should get our story straight?" Uncle Bob chimed in.

"Just tell them I was trying to protect some chick, and some guy hit me with a beer mug. I'll fill them in on the details later."

Armed with the shell of a coverup story, our heroes bid Matty adieu and headed to New Hyde Park to drop off The Big Man. Sitting in his darkened kitchen, The Big Man called Matty's dad, who was none too happy to receive this kind of news in the middle of the night. He explained that the entire incident was a freak accident (which it was) but left out every possible detail of the evening's actual events.

"Greg, are you telling me the truth," Matty's dad asked.

Without hesitation, The Big Man assured him it was just an accident and nothing more.

If I had to guess, he crossed his fingers the whole time.

Matty's dad arrived at the hospital soon after receiving the phone call. When asked what happened, Matty explained, "I was sitting at the bar, and a guy was yelling at some girl about something. I told him he should calm down. Then, I saw his reflection in the mirror; he was about to swing his beer mug at my head. I swiveled on the bar stool and raised my hand to block it."

It sounds plausible, right?

CHAPTER 8
THE AFTERMATH

The next day, Uncle Bob's father sleepily walked across the front lawn to retrieve the morning newspaper. Passing Bob's car in the driveway, he stopped and stared. Shaking his head, he returned to the house. Rustling Bob from a dead sleep, he asked what happened last night.

Bob struggled to lift his head from his pillow. "We just went out for a few drinks after work to celebrate my friend Paul's birthday."

"Really?" his father said. "Can you come outside for a minute?"

Bob foggily followed his dad, viewing the car for the first time in the daylight.

Blood was visible all over the side panel and on the front hood. It looked like he hit a deer. The back window, interior seats, and even the roof were covered in blood.

So, what happened to Matty, you ask?

After a few days, when released from the hospital, Matty walked out with a plastic bag containing the blue pinstriped suit he came in with. It was so full of blood that you couldn't see the pinstripes.

The doctor informed Matty that it would be about a year before he could return to normal activities. Matty told him, "That's for normal people. I've got a softball tournament on the Fourth of July, and I'm playing left field."

Matty wound up playing left field in the tournament.

EPILOGUE

So that's it, dear readers.

I hope some of these stories made you smile. They always make me smile.

As my wife read through the stories, she was concerned that they had the same basic theme: getting drunk and getting into trouble. Only the location and circumstances changed.

Well, that's what our lives were like back then.

Over the years, we all matured (to some degree) and found love and happiness with our own families. After reasonably successful careers, some of us retired, while others are still working.

I thought you might like to catch up with the cast of characters profiled in these stories.

BRUCE (MR. B)

Bruce (Mr. B) is a retired Healthcare IT Professional who lives in Mt. Sinai on Long Island with his wife, Chris. They have two wonderful children, Justin and Pamela. The happy couple became grandparents for the first time a few years ago when their daughter Pamela and her husband Antonio welcomed their son, Marco. Marco was joined by a new sister, Alessandra, in 2023.

Here's Bruce with Chris and his brother Peter:

EPILOGUE

GREG (THE BIG MAN)

Tragically, we lost the Big Man in January of 2024. Always a larger-than-life presence, he was a good friend, and I miss him terribly. Even in passing, his funeral provided a little comic relief. You see, his Fantasy Football Team, "Big Man's Hellhounds," won our league's championship in 2022. Part of the charm of our particular league (we started it back in 1981) is our trophy, the REMFL Cup (don't ask). Like hockey's Stanley Cup, the winner gets their name engraved on the trophy and takes possession of it for the year, much to the chagrin of their wives, I might add.

As commissioner, I take possession of the Cup after each season, engrave it, and present it to the new Champion. Here's a picture of the Big Man accepting the Cup in 2023.

Sadly, the Big Man passed before I could reclaim and engrave the Cup for next year's champion. We were supposed to meet for lunch the week after he died so I could get the trophy from him. To me, it was almost like an episode of *Curb Your Enthusiasm*, and I was Larry David. What do I say to his wife Linda at the funeral? "I'm so sorry we lost Greg; you must be devastated. By the way, where's the REMFL Cup?" What if it was in the coffin with him? I couldn't just reach in and grab it, could I?

To my surprise, Linda and their son Danny decided to display the cup at the funeral, along with pictures and other joyful things representing his life. They told me that winning that stupid trophy meant the world to him, which made me smile and weep at the same time.

God, I miss him so much…

EPILOGUE

THE DOWERS

Douglas Dower, who rose to the rank of Lieutenant in the Garden City Police Department before retiring, passed in 2020. He's survived by his wife Diane and their daughter Lauren. Diane still resides in Brightwaters on Long Island. Lauren lives in Arlington, Virginia, and works for a company that provides IT solutions to the Department of Defense and other State and Federal agencies.

Barbara Dower-Green retired from the Nassau County Police Department in 2010 as an Inspector. She also served as the Commanding Officer of the NCPD Police Academy. Interestingly enough, the Police Academy was located in Massapequa at the time of her appointment, in the former elementary school where she attended kindergarten. She told me that her office as CO was in the Principal's office.

She's currently living in Key West, Florida, but spends a lot of time with her sister Susan and her husband Richie in Plantation, Florida. Barbara sadly lost the love of her life, her husband Chris, in September of 2021. Both of their sons, Eddie and Mack, are Marine Engineers. Eddie and his wife Mary live in Virginia and expect their first child soon, making Barbara a Grandma (but don't call her that!). Mack and his Irish wife, Katie, live in Cork, Ireland. If you haven't already guessed, Barbara travels a lot these days.

Kerri Barr was Barbara's friend for most of her life before passing away in September 2013. She became a full-time mom right after her son Matt was born in 1995 and was proud to wear the title of "Hockey Mom," loving every minute of it.

We took these pictures in November 2011 after seeing Southside

Johnny at the Bolton Center in West Babylon, New York. There was a "Meet and Greet" after the show, and Barbara and Kerri met Southside for the first time that night.

Barbara and her husband Chris are on the left, with my brother Tony in front of them and Kerri to his right, with Southside over her left shoulder, his arm around her. I'm not sure who those other dudes photo-bombing the picture in the background were (lol).

The other is one of my favorites from that same evening, Kerri getting a hug from Southside Johnny.

EPILOGUE

MY BROTHER TONY

No matter how hard he tries, my brother Tony will always be four years younger than me, but as number two, he tries harder.

He and my sister-in-law Marina gave our family three kids: Michael, Caitlin, and Christopher. Although I may be the older brother, he has beaten me to the title of Grandpa many times over. Caitlin and her husband Mike got the ball rolling with Violet and June, Michael and Diedre followed up in January of 2024 with Anthony, while Christopher and Catherine are on track to make it four (another girl) at the end of the summer in 2024.

Between working as a director of supply chain for an Automotive-Industrial firm that caters to emergency services vehicles (yes, he's still working) and being a full-time Pop-Pop, he still finds time to enjoy fishing, cooking, and the occasional outing on the links.

This picture depicts two of his favorite pastimes, fishing and his grandkids.

JOHN COLQUHOUN

Besides attempting to steal pictures off walls and being a Southside Johnny fan, John became a highly acclaimed, award-winning illustrator with many local and national advertising campaigns, working for several New York City Ad Agencies. Originally from Long Island, he now lives in seclusion (just kidding) in upstate New York (Hillsdale) with his wife Linda, where he still roots for our New York Mets. They have three great kids: Alison, Jake, and Duncan. They recently became first-time grandparents with Sloane, thanks to Alison and her husband, Neil.

Since retiring from advertising, he began developing a comic strip, "The New 60," with Andy Landorf. The strip publishes new comics twice a week. You can find it on Facebook or online (www.thenew60-comic.com).

Oh yeah, he illustrated my first book, "Burning Through the West Coast," with drawings like this:

EPILOGUE

MATTY WYNN

Matty is a well-respected realtor on Long Island for over 35 years. He's married and currently living in a 55+ community in Suffolk County.

And yes, his wrist is still functional…

EPILOGUE

BOB BOCHICCHIO

Bob retired from his position as Director of Finance for the New York City Health and Hospital Corporations system a few years ago, where, for some reason, they put him in charge of billions of dollars a year in revenue. He and his wife, Brenda, relocated to a community called Citrus Hills in Florida in 2023. Their son Johnathan lives in the San Francisco Bay area with his fiancée, working in supply chain/inventory control for an internet retailer.

Also a long-time member of our fantasy football league, Bob's team, "Kickio's Korner," has won a record seven League Championships. However, if he wins another while living in Florida, he'll have to come up to NY to pick up the REMFL Cup.

In case I didn't make it clear, we're all still good friends, but we don't see each other nearly as often as we should. Hopefully, we can make up for lost time and share more war stories of our youth before we forget most of the details.

Like when we accidentally destroyed a hotel room in Springfield, Massachusetts, while I was covering a college basketball game for New York Tech as my photographer, Jim Gherardi, took pictures recording the mayhem. Or the time we got summonses for having an "open container" of beer while walking on the way to an Islander's playoff game and had to appear in front of a judge, where we pled, "Bochicchio." There was Mr. B's bachelor party and an ill-fated trip in a rented station wagon to a bar in New Jersey called Jimmy Byrne's.

Oh, wait—what about Thanksgiving night at the Dower's house or when we spent a full day at Freehold Racetrack in New Jersey for an outdoor concert?

I could go on and on.

Maybe someday, I will…

ABOUT THE AUTHOR

Paul DiSclafani is an award-winning newspaper columnist currently published in local newspapers across Nassau County on Long Island, in New York. His column "Long Island Living" has garnered several writing awards.

The Press Club of Long Island has awarded "Long Island Living" Media Awards every year since he began writing the column back in 2017. In 2021, PCLI voted Long Island Living the best column published on Long Island.

A Massapequa resident since 1967, Paul grew up in the East New York section of Brooklyn, surrounded by a large Italian family. Many of his columns and musings recall family gatherings and touch on all aspects of life today.

Paul began his love affair with the printed word after taking a journalism class during his senior year in high school. That led to a successful writing career in college as a sportswriter and editor. Although pursuing a career in Healthcare IT, he continued to make friends and colleagues chuckle with stories and tales (both written and verbal) throughout the years.

He retired as a Healthcare IT Professional in January of 2024.

Having told stories over the years of adventures with his friends and even chronicling them in short story form, he decided to finally sit down and write a book about one of them. *Burning Through the West Coast*, his first book, was published by Red Penguin Books in October of 2020.

In 2021, Red Penguin published a collection of his favorite Long Island Living columns called *A View From the Bench*. Several of his columns and stories have also been published in other collections. Visit his website at www.pauldisclafani.com for a complete listing of all his published works. You can also subscribe to his monthly newsletter on the web page.

A married father of two, Paul and his wife Barbara have been blessed with two great kids, James and Kevin. They became in-laws when Kevin married Arielle Dagger in July of 2022.

From left to right: Kevin, Arielle, Ellyn, and James.

WRITING AWARDS:

- 2018 Press Club of Long Island: Narrative-Column (Third Place) "Long Island Living"
- 2020 Press Club of Long Island: Narrative-Column (Second Place) "Long Island Living"
- 2020 Press Club of Long Island: Narrative-Humor (Third Place) "My Stupid House"
- 2020 New York Press Association: Best Humor Column (Third Place) "Long Island Living"
- 2021 Press Club of Long Island: Narrative-Column (First Place) "Long Island Living"
- 2021 Press Club of Long Island: Narrative-Humor (Second Place) "A Few Hours at the DMV"
- 2022 Press Club of Long Island: Narrative-Humor (Second Place) "The Day Before"
- 2023 Press Club of Long Island: Narrative-Humor (Second Place) "I'm Still a Man, Right?"
- 2024 Press Club of Long Island: Narrative-Humor (Third Place) "Are You Ready for Human Composting?"

ALSO BY PAUL DISCLAFANI

PUBLICATIONS

Burning Through the West Coast
6,000 Miles, 576 Beers, 4 States, 3 Guys from the East Coast ... and a Bag of Weed

Red Penguin, 2020

Long Island Living
A Journey Through the Mind of a Newspaper Columnist

Red Penguin, 2021

CONTRIBUTIONS TO COLLECTIONS

"Vacationing With and Without the Kids"
A Trip for the Books
Edited by JK Larkin
A Red Penguin Collection, 2020

"I'm Not Prepared for the Apocalypse"
It's the End of the World
Edited by JK Larkin
A Red Penguin Collection, 2020

"A Trip to Jungleland"
Anthology
Long Island Authors Group Publishing, 2022

"Just Another Day at the Park"

Backyards to Ballparks

Edited by Eric C Gray

Palmetto Publishing, 2022

www.ingramcontent.com/pod-product-compliance
Lightning Source LLC
Chambersburg PA
CBHW072154070526
44585CB00015B/1133